THE PRAYERS OF THE NEW TESTAMENT

THE PRAYERS OF THE
NEW TESTAMENT

DONALD COGGAN
Archbishop of Canterbury

1817

HARPER & ROW, PUBLISHERS
New York, Evanston, San Francisco, London

STANDARD BOOK NUMBER: 0-06-061511-7

LIBRARY OF CONGRESS CATALOG CARD NUMBER: 74-25683

Dedicated to

CAREY FREDERICK KNYVETT	Bishop of Selby, 1941-1962
GEORGE FREDERICK TOWNLEY	Bishop of Hull, 1957-1965
GEORGE D'OYLY SNOW	Bishop of Whitby, 1961
DOUGLAS NOEL SARGENT	Bishop of Selby, 1962
HUBERT LAURENCE HIGGS	Bishop of Hull, 1965

οὓς ἐγὼ ἀγαπῶ ἐν ἀληθείᾳ

PREFACE

For many years I have wanted to write this book but have been hindered from doing so. Pressure of work has been one factor in hindering me, and a sense of unworthiness another. Who am I to write a book on prayer? Certainly I am no expert. It is 'not as though I had already attained either were already perfect' in an art which has taxed the saints of the ages and elicited a vast literature of its own. But perhaps this 'hindrance' is in itself something of a reason for the writing of this book. It is for the ordinary man and woman—the people who are told, and who in varying degrees believe, that prayer is an important part of the spiritual life and who would be prepared to go at it seriously if only they knew how. Some have read books on prayer, but have found them, as the Psalmist found God's knowledge of him, 'too wonderful and excellent for' them, they 'cannot attain unto it'! Others have read no books on the subject, but they stumble along, sometimes tempted to abandon the effort, sometimes glimpsing the fact that they are at the beginning of a road which would lead to a fair country if only someone would guide them. They do not need more exhortation to pray. They need direction and exposition.

Such ordinary men and women I have had in mind; and in addition I have thought of that great band of Readers to whom the Church owes so much. Sunday by Sunday they preach and conduct the services. But how arid will that ministry become if it is not watered by a life of prayer! Often, too, they will want to teach their congregations about the meaning of prayer—what shall they say? Then, too, there are Fellowship groups of various kinds, meeting to discover more of the meaning of Christian discipleship. I have had them in mind.

Perhaps it is not too much to hope that some clergy and women workers, too, may find here a stimulus, if not to their own life of prayer, then to their exposition of it to their people.

This book is one of straightforward exposition. I have taken all the prayers recorded in the New Testament, and have tried simply and faithfully to expound them in such a way as to incite the reader to kneel down and thoughtfully make the prayers his own. I have excluded the *Magnificat*, for it is a Psalm of exultation rather than a prayer, and the *Benedictus*, which is 'prophecy' (*St. Luke* 1:67). New Testament experts will find that many points of critical interest and importance have sometimes been altogether by-passed or else been but briefly touched on. The reason for such scant treatment is in order not to divert attention from the main point of the prayer.

Many of the prayers are so rich in content that it will be found best to take a small section, both of the prayer and of the exposition, at a time, and refuse to go on until the reader has made time to meditate and to make the prayer his own. This is not a book for hurried reading 'at a sitting'. Rather it is aimed for use over a longish period—to be taken in daily doses and then gone over again! Thus, the Lord's Prayer is divided into eight sections, and should take at least as many days. Then another day or two will be called for, to see the prayer as whole and to learn to say it, thoughtfully, in its entirety. What is true of the Lord's Prayer will be found to be true also of the prayers of St. Paul, who has an uncanny way of packing vast wealth into a tiny compass.

The fact that the book is intended not for hurried reading but as a basis for meditation accounts for the rather ample Scriptural references which I have given, as also for the cross-references in the book itself. The fact that, on the whole, the comments towards the end of the book are briefer than in the earlier part is due to there being no need to repeat notes on concepts dealt with previously—a reference is all that is needed. I have made use of a variety of versions, and sometimes have given renderings of my own.

In November 1964 I had the privilege of delivering the Louisa Curtis Lectures at Spurgeon's College, London; and in May 1966 the McMath Lectures in the Diocese of Michigan. On these occasions I used material which is now part of this book. To kindly audiences who allowed me to 'try out' some of these chapters on them, I owe my thanks. And to generous hosts and to multitudes of friends made on these excursions, I tender my gratitude, especially to Principal G. R. Beasley-Murray at Spurgeon's College, and to Bishop R. S. M. Emrich and Dean L. G. Warren at Detroit.

I am grateful to my wife for her constant encouragement and for her making of the index, to Mrs. N. Charlton for her patient and accurate typing and to Mr. D. Blunt for reading the proofs.

One of John Baillie's most delightful and helpful books is called *Invitation to Pilgrimage*. This book is just that—an invitation to the pilgrimage of prayer. In so far as the reading of each section leads the reader to kneel and make the prayer his own, so far the book will have succeeded in its purpose.

DONALD CANTUAR:

Canterbury

CONTENTS

CONTENTS

Let thy merciful ears, O Lord, be open to the prayers of thy humble servants; and that they may obtain their petitions make them to ask such things as shall please thee; through Jesus Christ our Lord. Amen.

(Collect of the tenth Sunday after Trinity)

We think him not safe who is undefended by the arms and the guard of prayer.

(Bishop Lancelot Andrewes, *Prayers*)

ABBREVIATIONS

A.V.	Authorised Version (1611)
Moffatt	A New Translation of the Bible (1926, revised 1935)
N.E.B.	New English Bible: New Testament (1961)
Phillips	The New Testament in Modern English. J. B. Phillips (1958)
P.B.V.	Psalms (Prayer Book Version)
Revised Psalter	The text produced by the Archbishops' Commission to revise the Psalter, authorised for use in public worship (1966)
R.S.V.	Revised Standard Version (1952)
R.V.	Revised Version (N.T. 1881, O.T. 1885)
Rieu	The Four Gospels: A New Translation (1952)

THE PRAYERS IN THE GOSPELS

THE prayers in this section are mostly prayers of our Lord to His Father (not exclusively so, for we shall study the prayers of the Blessed Virgin Mary and of the aged Simeon, in the opening chapters of St. Luke). The main purpose of this book is to study the prayers themselves as a stimulus to our thinking and a pattern for our devotion. But it would be well, first, to watch our Lord at the work of prayer before we study the form of the words He used. There is a good deal in the Gospels which is helpfully suggestive here.

It should be noted that in the use of the word 'prayer' I do not include the address of contemporaries to the incarnate Christ (for example, that of the blind man, 'Son of David, have mercy on me').

The Gospels clearly indicate that the life of Jesus was one of hard toil and that during His ministry He was under constant pressure from thronging crowds. Few things are more exhausting than life lived in the glare of publicity. Nor, we must assume, did Jesus ever heal without power going out of Him (see, for example, *St. Mark* 5: 30). Being very man, it 'took it out of Him' to minister to the needs, spiritual, mental and physical, of those who daily pressed in on Him.

Let us look at a typical passage in the first chapter of St. Mark. The conflict of the forces of wholeness and light with the demonic powers of darkness centred in the Person of Jesus (vv. 32-34). We see here no placid Galilaean poet meditating amid flower-covered hills. We see, instead, God's 'proper Man' doing battle with all that mars human life – and winning in the fray. Then St. Mark sketches the story of the disciples going in pursuit of their Master, bringing Him the message that everybody was looking for Him (vv. 36-37). He hints at the passion that burned within our Lord to preach throughout the length and breadth of Galilee in fulfilment of His mission (vv. 38-39). But between these two little accounts is a passage of the deepest significance – 'Very early next morning' (i.e. after His healing work) 'He got up and went out. He went away to a lonely spot and remained there in prayer' (v. 35, N.E.B.).

'He got up' – no lying in bed beyond the time really necessary for bodily refreshment. 'He went out' – out of the small house where every step would be heard – 'to a lonely spot'. He could not carry on a ministry of constant self-giving without such renewal. He knew *where* to find this – in the open country, alone with God. He knew *when* to find it – in the early morning, before the crowds were up and doing. With that behind Him, He could face anything.

Look at another passage in St. Mark. In chapter 6, the evangelist gives the story of the feeding of the five thousand (vv. 33-44). Intense activity, considerable excitement, milling crowds again! Then the story of the storm on the lake, with the disciples terrified by the storm itself and by the appearance of One whom they took to be a ghost (vv. 47 ff.). How did the Lord keep His serenity in the midst of that? The answer is given in v. 46 – 'He bade them farewell, and then withdrew into the hills to pray' (E.V. Rieu's translation). Withdrawal with God gave Him peace within and a serenity infectious to others. In the presence of God He held Himself still, and so had reserves of power which enabled Him to stretch out a firm hand to those who were finding life too much for them. At a time of intense activity, Martin Luther wrote: 'I am so busy that I find I cannot do with less than four hours a day in the presence of God'.

Thus there would seem to have been a kind of rhythm about the life of Jesus – withdrawal and work; withdrawal and work. It was a rhythm which he sought to teach to His apostles, as St. Mark makes plain in this same chapter (6: 30 ff.). They had been out on their Master's errands, and now they came back to report to Him all they had done and taught. No comment of His is recorded, but simply the fact that He told them they must withdraw and rest. He went with them for that vital period of renewal which He needed; and if He, how much more they!

Let us watch Him again. He is faced with a great decision, the choice of twelve men to be the main pillars of the Christian Church at the very beginning (*St. Luke* 6: 12 ff.). What vast issues hung on the choice of that heterogeneous group! One cannot but suppose that this matter had been on His mind for a very long time. Probably He had grown up in the companionship of some at least of these men. Now the day was coming when from among that bigger band of His disciples He must call out twelve to be apostles. Behind that momentous choice, no doubt, lay months, perhaps years, of steady prayer directed to this end. But in addition to this, there was the intense, concentrated prayer of a whole night spent in the mountains with God (v. 12).

This would suggest that the right background for special prayer in an emergency is the steady habit of daily prayer from which our knowledge of God grows. He who knows God in the intimacy gained from daily intercourse will not lack guidance when, in an emergency or faced by a weighty decision, he turns to Him for special direction.

Yet again we watch Him. He is instituting the Last Supper (*St. Mark* 14: 22 ff.). The story is told very simply and with considerable solemnity. Yet it is shot through with praise and thanksgiving. Two words are used for the 'blessing' (v. 22) and the 'giving thanks' (v. 23), words which we know in their English dress as 'eulogy' and 'eucharist'. 'The Blessing... is an act of thanksgiving to God, and, according to Jewish usage, would take the form: "Praised be Thou, O Lord our God, King of the Universe, who bringest forth bread from the earth", or ... "Blessed art Thou, our Father in heaven, who givest us today the bread necessary for us" ' (V. Taylor, *The Gospel according to St. Mark*, p. 544). It is likely that it had long been the habit of Jesus to preface His meals with His Apostles by some such 'grace' as this, and He did it again before instituting that meal which for millions down the centuries has been the heart of their devotion and one of the chief means of strength for their spiritual life.

The meal is followed by the singing of a hymn (v. 26). This hymn is generally held to be the second part of what is called the *Hallel* (*Psalms* 115-118). Against that background of thanksgiving and praise is set the stern drama of the Passion and of the redemption of the world by the laying down of the life of the Son of God.

ST. MATTHEW

St. Matthew 6: 9-13

A.V.	N.E.B.
9. Our Father which art in heaven, Hallowed be thy name.	'Our Father in heaven, Thy name be hallowed;
10. Thy kingdom come. Thy will be done in earth, as it is in heaven.	Thy kingdom come, Thy will be done, On earth as in heaven.
11. Give us this day our daily bread.	Give us today our daily bread.
12. And forgive us our debts, as we forgive our debtors.	Forgive us the wrong we have done, As we have forgiven those who have wronged us.
13. And lead us not into temptation, but deliver us from evil: For thine is the kingdom, and the power, and the glory, for ever. Amen.	And do not bring us to the test, But save us from the evil one.'

The parallel passage in St. Luke runs:

St. Luke 11: 2-4

A.V.	N.E.B.
2. Our Father which art in heaven, Hallowed be thy name. Thy kingdom come. Thy will be done, as in heaven, so in earth.	'Father, thy name be hallowed; Thy kingdom come.
3. Give us day by day our daily bread.	Give us each day our daily bread.
4. And forgive us our sins; for we also forgive every one that is indebted to us. And lead us not into temptation; but deliver us from evil.	And forgive us our sins, For we too forgive all who have done us wrong. And do not bring us to the test.'

Our Father which art in heaven

St. Luke hints that it was the sight of Jesus at prayer that made one of His disciples ask for instruction as to how to set about it.

'. . . Jesus was at prayer. When He ceased, one of His disciples said, "Lord, teach us . . ." ' (11: 1, N.E.B.). There had been the example of John Baptist and his teaching of his followers. But the immediate reason behind the request was the example of Jesus Himself. That is suggestive. A prayerful life, with a character to match, is a better invitation to prayer than many exhortations.

Our Lord knew that to learn how to pray, how to enter into the secret place of the Most High, was the most important lesson any man could learn. He was quick to answer the request, and in so doing gave His enquirer the disciples' prayer, which we know as the Lord's Prayer.

The seeds of most of the great themes of the teaching of Jesus are to be found in the Old Testament. It was His genius to take the tiny thing, to extend it, develop it, stretch it, elaborate its implications. This was true supremely of His teaching about God. He spoke of Him mainly in two ways:

First, He spoke of God as King. He saw in God kingly rule and authority. Of this the Old Testament frequently spoke – 'The Lord is King, the earth may be glad thereof' (*Psalms* 97: 1, P.B.V.); 'How beautiful upon the mountains are the feet of him that . . . saith unto Zion, Thy God reigneth!' (*Isaiah* 52: 7). Such passages are legion. Jesus took up the theme, and

> 'In His hands the thing became a trumpet
> Whence He blew soul-animating strains'.

At the centre of His teaching was the reign, the kingly rule, of God.

Secondly, He spoke of God as Father. Here again the springs of His teaching are to be found in the Old Testament. Sometimes the Father-son relationship is thought of in national terms, sometimes in individual; it is an important concept in the Israelitish thought of God. So the Psalmist could write: 'Like as a father pitieth his own children: even so is the Lord merciful unto them that fear Him' (*Psalms* 103: 13, P.B.V.). And Malachi could exclaim 'Have we not all one father? hath not one God created us?' (2: 10). Hosea, in a moving passage, called Israel the *son* of God: 'When Israel was a child, then I loved him, and called my son out of Egypt' (11: 1). The later chapters of Isaiah return several times to this thought: 'Thou, O Lord, art our father; our redeemer from of old is Thy name' (63: 16, following George Adam Smith's translation in *The Book of Isaiah*, Vol. 2, p. 492). 'Now, O Lord, Thou art our father; we are the clay, and Thou our potter; and we all are the work of Thy hand' (64: 8). And even in passages where Father-son vocabulary is not actually used, the thought comes very close to it; for example, 'I the Eternal your God hold you by the hand, whispering: "Fear not, I will help you" ' (*Isaiah* 41: 13, Moffatt).

Jesus took up the theme, elaborating and intensifying it in passage after passage of His teaching, perhaps reaching the climax of perfection in that parable of the prodigal son, which is better called the parable of the prodigal Father, since he poured out his love on one who was wholly undeserving of it.

But it was not only in His verbal teaching that Jesus bore His witness to the truth of the Fatherhood of God. His own personal experience, in so far as it is disclosed to us in the pages of the Gospels, shows how central was this concept to His thinking and devotion. Little is known of Joseph who in the early years of Jesus' life acted as a father to Him. But we may guess that the relationship between man and Boy was such that Joseph made it easy for Jesus to think of God as Father and to teach about Him as such. Jesus saw a reflection of the Old Testament teaching about God as Father in the person of him who stood in the relation of father to Him in the Nazareth home.

Perhaps it is significant that the only story which has come down to us in the Gospels about the childhood of Jesus has to do with a conflict of loyalties in the mind of Jesus — loyalty to the Heavenly Father *or* loyalty to Joseph and Mary. However the phrase in *St. Luke* 2: 49 be translated ('about My Father's business' or 'in My Father's house' or 'among My Father's people'), it is clear that our Lord knew, even in that early stage of His development, the demanding nature of His divine sonship. This intimate, personal relationship involved claims on Him which were absolute and could brook no refusal.

St. Luke's version of the Lord's Prayer begins with the simple word 'Father'. (It is only inferior manuscripts and versions which have the expanded form here, 'Our Father in heaven'.) This was the usual form in which Jesus addressed God. 'Now this word *Abba*, used in prayer, was something new. In the prayers of antique Judaism this invocation of God is not to be found. Why should this be so? The Church Fathers, Chrysostom, Theodore, and Theodoret, who came from wealthy families of Antioch and probably had Aramaic-speaking nurses, tell us that *abba* was the word used by a small child when addressing his father . . . *Abba* was a homely familial expression, the tender address of the baby to his father: "father dear" — a secular word.' So writes Professor J. Jeremias. It is highly significant that in a world whose language was predom-

inantly Greek, this word *abba* so impressed itself on the minds of
the early Christians that they held on to it, even when they had to
accompany it with a translation into their own tongue. Here was
the survival of one of the very words of Jesus, from the heart of His
prayer-life, and they would not let it go (see *St. Mark* 14: 36;
Galatians 4: 6; *Romans* 8: 15). Even at the end of His earthly life,
when He was *in extremis*, Jesus used the familiar form of address,
prefacing it to a sentence from the Psalms – 'Father, into Thy hands
I commend My spirit' (*St. Luke* 23: 46, quoting *Psalms* 31: 5).

This intimacy of spiritual relationship, experienced in unique
fashion by our Lord and elaborated in His teaching, is of great
importance in our own generation. We are subject, to a degree in
which former generations were not, to what has been called
'astronomical intimidation'. Ours is an expanding universe, and
every discovery of the astronomers makes our imagination reel at
its vastness. Where does man come into the picture? And what is
God like? Can we do no more than describe Him in neuter terms as
that which is? Or should we think of Him just as the Creator Who
set the huge machine in motion or, at best, as a kind of managing
director of a great concern who cannot be bothered with the
problems of a junior office-boy? Robert Louis Stevenson's words –

> 'The world is so big and I am so small,
> I do not like it at all, at all ――'

find an echo in the minds of many a modern man. At the heart of
the universe Jesus teaches us to see One Who can best be thought
of in terms of fatherly love and kingly authority, One without
Whom not a sparrow falls to the ground, our *Father*.

Here in this concept, then, is *intimacy*. But there is more. Here
is *majesty* also – 'our Father *which art in heaven*'. Here is no hand-
shaking relationship with God. Here is no sentimentality in
religion. Here is no grandfather in heaven whose only concern it is
(as C. S. Lewis put it) that at the end of the day it should be said
that a good time was had by all! In Judaism fatherhood implied
authority. In twentieth-century England a youngster may call his
father 'Pop'. It is hardly likely that that was done in Palestine in
the first century. There is something awe-inspiring in the phrase
'which art in heaven'. 'God is in heaven, and thou upon earth:
therefore let thy words be few' – it was a timely warning which the
ancient writer gave (*Ecclesiastes* 5: 2). This sense of the holiness
and majesty of God is the antiseptic element in our religion which
saves it from lapsing into an easy-going sentimentalism.

The phrase is a reminder that he who would come into the presence of God can only come as a worshipping sinner. For in worship I hold myself, sinner that I am, to attention in the presence of the all-holy; weak as I am, in the presence of the all-mighty; ignorant as I am, in the presence of the all-knowing. I press my sinfulness close to His forgiveness, my weakness to His strength, my ignorance to His wisdom. I come in silence, ready to wait on the God who speaks and who is always there before me. I come in awe to the God of majesty. C. S. Lewis in his correspondence with 'Malcolm' writes:

> 'I fully agree that the relationship between God and a man is more private and intimate than any possible relation between two fellow creatures. Yes, but at the same time there is, in another way, a greater distance between the participants. We are approaching—well I won't say "the Wholly Other", for I suspect that is meaningless, but the Unimaginably and Insupportably Other. We ought to be—sometimes I hope one is—simultaneously aware of closest proximity and infinite distance. You make things far too snug and confiding. Your erotic analogy needs to be supplemented by "I fell at His feet as one dead"' (*Letters to Malcolm Chiefly on Prayer*, p. 23).

St. Peter put it in a nutshell: 'If you say "our Father" to the One who judges every man impartially on the record of his deeds, you must stand in awe of him while you live out your time on earth' (1 *Peter* 1: 17, N.E.B.).

'Our courteous Lord', wrote the Lady Julian of Norwich, 'willeth that we should be as homely with Him as heart may think or soul may desire. But let us beware that we take not so recklessly this homeliness that we leave courtesy. For our Lord Himself is sovereign homeliness, and as homely as He is, so courteous He is: for He is very courteous.' By 'courteous', she meant 'gracious'; by 'homely', 'intimate'. In these words in her *Revelations of Divine Love*, she redresses a balance all too often upset.

I come, too, as a member of a worshipping community, sharing in corporate need. I do not pray 'my Father' but 'our Father' – and this in a twofold sense.

First, there is a sense in which the fatherhood of God embraces the whole world. He causes His sun to shine on just and unjust alike. 'God so loved the *world* . . .' The love and compassion of God go out to His entire creation. (This great doctrine has as its corollary the doctrine of the brotherhood of man; if God is Father of all and I am His child, all men are my brethren.) Hence springs the Christian hatred of all barriers of race, of segregation, of anything which degrades personality or uses persons as the mere means of another's pleasure. Hence springs the Christian concern over social issues, and the Christian participation in reforms that make for the total welfare of persons as persons. Hence springs the Christian conviction that involvement in social issues is part and parcel of what it means to be a Christian disciple.

But *secondly*, in a deeper and more limited sense, God can only be the Father of those who respond to His love, and of those who, in obedience to Him, are willing to share in the discipline of the life of His family, the Church. Indeed one must say that the idea of the Church is implicit in the idea of the divine Fatherhood. This doctrine is no 'optional extra' added on by a later generation to the originally simple teaching of the Galilaean prophet. Fatherhood implies a family; and a family implies obligations, and a family Table. 'When ye pray, say, "Our Father" '.

So the Master taught. So the Master teaches. So we falteringly learn.

'Lord, teach us to pray'
'Our Father which art in heaven . . .'

Hallowed be Thy name

The name is the *person*. So at least a Hebrew thought when he used the word. ('Thou hast a few *names* even in Sardis which have not defiled their garments' (*Revelation* 3: 4). This simply means a few *people*.) Thus the Name of God is the essential being of God—

> 'God's presence and His very self
> And essence all-Divine' ——

as J. H. Newman put it.

What does it mean to hallow the name of God? Truth can often be seen by looking at the opposite of a statement or phrase. So we may ask: 'What did it mean to a Biblical writer to desecrate the name of God? How did he conceive that it could be defiled, dishonoured, or treated as though it were not sacred?' No doubt very often in Jewish history it was thought that the name of God was desecrated if some ritual taboo was disobeyed—if a prescribed sacrifice was not offered or if a corpse was touched. But the prophets taught, in many a stinging phrase, that it was possible to be ritually correct and at the same time ethically wrong and in *this* way the name of God was desecrated.

23

The third commandment had originally little if anything to do with the use of what we call 'bad language'. To 'take the name of the Lord thy God in vain' was to fail in the ethical duty of keeping a vow or fulfilling an obligation solemnly made to one's neighbour. If, conversely, such an obligation was kept, then the name of God was hallowed.

The name of God is desecrated when the poor are crushed, when a widow is denied her rights, when unjust scales are used in commerce, when sexual immorality takes place (see, for example, *Amos* 2: 7, R.S.V. — 'a man and his father go in to the same maiden, so that My holy name is profaned'). But when the name of God is hallowed all facets of everyday life and ethics are affected. 'To take God's name "in vain" is to refuse to take seriously the claim of God to command our obedience in social, political and economic affairs as well as in our private lives' (William Neil, *One Volume Bible Commentary*, p. 91).

In His high-priestly prayer (*St. John* 17) our Lord takes us one step further in the discovery of the meaning of this clause in the prayer. He 'hallowed the name of the Father by *manifesting* it (v. 6), by *declaring* it (v. 26). That is to say, He spent His life showing men what God is like. When men saw Him in His powerful beauty, they saw the Father. A Christlike character is the best way of hallowing the name of God.

You have some great task to do, some great decision to make. You begin it with the prayer, 'hallowed be Thy name'; you complete it with the *Gloria*, 'Glory be to the Father and to the Son and to the Holy Ghost'. That task, that decision, will not be far from the will and purpose of God.

You have some small task to do with hand or brain, a letter to write, a visit to pay, a chore to labour at. You begin with 'hallowed be Thy name'; you end with the *Gloria*. It will become an act of worship.

F. T. Palgrave got near the mark in his hymn: 'O Thou not made with hands' —

> 'Where'er the gentle heart
> Finds courage from above;
> Where'er the heart forsook
> Warms with the breath of love,
> Where faith bids fear depart,
> City of God, thou art' —

Yes, and there the Name of God is hallowed.

'Where in life's common ways
With cheerful feet we go;
Where in His steps we tread,
Who trod the way of woe;
Where He is in the heart,
City of God, thou art'—

Yes, and there the Name of God is hallowed.

Thy kingdom come

The Kingdom in Jewish thought means the reign, the sovereignty, of God. To pray this prayer is to pray for the suppression of whatever forces oppose the fulfilment of His will and purpose. When we pray these three words, we ask that, in the conflict between good and evil in the world, God's supremacy may be seen, His sovereignty manifested.

To pray this prayer is to ask for something wider than the extension of the Church. It is a mistake to think of Church and Kingdom as synonymous. They are not. It is truer to think of the Church as the agent of the Kingdom.

The sovereignty of God may be advanced, the Kingdom may 'come', through those who are unconscious of being its agents. The *scientist* who, while acknowledging no allegiance to God, makes inroads against the forces of disease, is, unwittingly, advancing the Kingdom. The *politician* who lays the foundations of a peaceful society is advancing the Kingdom, inasmuch as God is a God of order and of peace, rather than of confusion and war. We may regret it—we do regret it—if that politician is not a committed Christian. We may hold—we do hold—that if he were to lay his foundations on securely Christian principles, his building would be the surer. But in so far as the forces of peace and truth are strengthened by his endeavours, so far is the Kingdom advanced. The *writer* who, though not a Christian, writes beautiful and clean prose or poetry, advances the Kingdom. Wherever the bounds of beauty, truth and goodness are advanced, there the Kingdom comes. Wherever the forces of darkness, disease and hate are driven back, there the Kingdom comes, and God enters in more fully to the sovereignty of His world.

The prayer 'Thy kingdom come', therefore, can be answered through those who are not consciously the agents of the Kingdom. But, of course, this prayer is the prayer of the Church. Here is expressed our great longing. As the Church goes on its *evangelistic* errand, it prays for the coming of the Kingdom in the conversion of the careless; as the Church goes on its *teaching* mission, it prays for the coming of the Kingdom in driving back areas of intellectual darkness; as the Church goes on its *healing* mission, it prays for the coming of the Kingdom in the mastery of the forces of sickness and disease.

We, the members of the Body of Christ, are deeply and inextricably involved in the world of which we are part, and for which Christ died. We cannot 'contract out', for He did not contract out. With Him we bear something of the load of the world's sorrow and sin and ignorance and disease.

As we look around at a sick world, we pray: 'Thy kingdom come' — and we roll up our sleeves and go to it!

The prayer, however, is more than a this-worldly one. It is an eschatological prayer. That is to say, it reaches out beyond the confines of this age and of this world-order to the beyond. On the one hand, it is true that the Christian finds himself deeply engaged in the problems of a sin-ridden society and the ills of a sick world, for his Master's ministry was an engagement with sin, ignorance and disease. But on the other hand, and in the midst of the battle, the Christian looks up and looks forward — up to the God Who reigns, and forward to the day when that reign shall be manifested in its fulness. 'For He must reign, till He hath put all enemies under His feet' (1 *Corinthians* 15: 25).

As he toils and battles, the Christian disciple prays — and sings — because he knows the victory will be won. Indeed it is won already. In the life and death and resurrection of Jesus, the powers of the age to come have invaded this world-order. The enemy's death-sentence has been pronounced.

So, day by day, the Church prays in solemn, joyful hope and in confident expectation: 'Thy kingdom come'. 'Even so, come, Lord Jesus.' 'For thine is the kingdom . . .'

Thy will be done in earth, as it is in heaven

Where did the Boy Jesus learn to pray? It would not be a rash reply to suggest that He learnt at the knees of Joseph and Mary. The atmosphere of that humble home was such, the relationship between Joseph and Mary, and between them and the children in the family was such, that it seemed natural to kneel to pray together.

What about this particular clause in the Prayer? Is it not likely that Mary herself had a special share in teaching her Son how to pray it? For she herself had prayed it in her own way at her moment of crisis, if not in so many words then certainly in essence. 'Behold the handmaid of the Lord; be it unto me according to Thy word' (*St. Luke* 1: 38). He learned the lesson at least in part from her; and when His great moment of crisis came, He knew how to pray in an agony in the garden: 'Thy will be done' (*St. Matthew* 26: 42). His was the great assent, the great 'Yes' to the will of God, as hers had been.

She had interpreted her assent in terms of servant-hood. 'Behold the hand-maid, the servant, the slave of the Lord', she had said. There is nothing lower or more abject than a slave. He, or she, must be ready for anything at any time. As it had been with Mary, so it was with her Son, though in greater and fuller fashion and in more complete obedience.

What He learnt at His mother's knee of the meaning of being a servant of the Lord He found elaborated in Isaiah's pictures of the suffering servant (especially in chs. 42: 1-4; 49: 1-6; 50: 4-9; 52: 13-53: 12). These passages deserve careful study in a modern version. It would seem that Jesus fed His mind and soul on them and interpreted His mission as Messiah in the light of them. When the great temptation came to Him in the wilderness (*St. Matthew* 4: 1-11; *St. Luke* 4: 1-13), it came in the form of a temptation to interpret His mission in terms of power and popularity ('Give the people food, fun and freedom'). Thrice He was tempted. Thrice He refused the temptation. He was to be the Servant of the Lord and the Servant of His people. Only so could He redeem, restore, rescue. Messiahship was to be worked out in terms of love and service and sacrifice. The rest of the Gospel story is but a comment on this initial decision. 'Behold the Servant of the Lord.' 'Thy will be done', Thy heart disclosed, Thy mind interpreted, in those terms.

The unknown author of the Epistle to the Hebrews elaborated this theme, especially in chapter 10. 'It was not the death of Jesus but His willingness to die which pleased the Father' – so wrote St. Bernard (*non mors placuit, sed voluntas sponte morientis*). 'Sacrifice and offering thou wouldest not, but a body hast thou prepared me' (v. 5) – that sacred body which the Blessed Virgin had her share in creating. So He had an instrument, a vehicle of personality, which He could offer, in its unblemished wholeness, to the Father – 'Lo, I come to do Thy will, O God' (v. 9). His will and the Father's were one. 'And it is by this *will* that we are consecrated, because Jesus Christ once for all has *offered* up His *body*' (10: 10, Moffatt).

27

The prayer of consent: the prayer of assent: my 'Yes' to the divine will. What does that mean? It does *not* mean a meek and flabby assent to the *status quo*, a resigned 'God wills it' when 'it' may be due to man's stupidity or crass carelessness. When little children die because drains are bad or the food inadequate, the Christian does not murmur 'God wills it'. He gets up and fights foul conditions. His Master was a fighter even to the death. 'This woman . . . *whom Satan hath bound*' (*St. Luke* 13: 16) was His description of the woman with the crooked back. 'An enemy hath done this' (*St. Matthew* 13: 28); and that enemy must be fought and defeated, whether the enemy be sin or ignorance or sickness or a combination of them all. The prayer of assent will undoubtedly mean the allying of ourselves with the great warrior Christ, to do battle with His enemies. And if that means hurt or long hours, or little respite, we need not be surprised.

> 'Captain belovèd, battle wounds were Thine;
> Let me not wonder if some hurt be mine.
> Rather, O Lord, let this my wonder be
> That I may share a battle wound with Thee.'
>
> (Amy Carmichael)

But the prayer – and the life – of assent works out in subtler ways than those of battle. There is a thrill in doing battle, even if the wounds hurt and the flesh craves for rest. But there are other situations in which our Lord looks to us for the prayer of assent – 'be it unto me according to Thy will'. I mention one.

There are times in the spiritual life when we cry out for some evidence, some token, however small, of the nearness of God, of the presence of Christ. 'If only', we say, 'for one moment He would rend the veil, and for one moment the walk of faith might be turned to the wonder of sight.' If only God 'would sign His sunsets, as Turner did' (I owe the phrase to Paul Scherer, *The Word God Sent*, p. 29). But no; it does not happen. Doubt assails us (and we are tempted to forget that there is a big difference between doubt and sin). Depression attacks us. 'Oh that Thou wouldest rend the heavens, that thou wouldest come down' (*Isaiah* 64: 1). Just a glimpse of reality, and we could go on our way reassured and refreshed. But no glimpse is vouchsafed. Perhaps this is especially the temptation of the middle years or of the after-middle years of life. The 'first fine careless rapture' of discipleship is over. We are in the long, straight stretch when endurance, that very humdrum virtue, is called for! We have our bereavements, and there are gaps in the family circle. It is then that God looks to us for our assent. 'Lord, if that is Thy way for me, behold the servant, the handmaid of the Lord: be it unto me according to Thy will.' That will work out in steady continuance – in prayer, in sacrament, in Bible study, in *service*. That way there will be no souring, no embitterment, but, rather, a deepening of the spiritual life. That way, God will fashion a servant, a handmaid, more after His own pattern, until the day dawns when faith gives way to sight, and 'His servants shall worship Him; they shall see Him face to face' (*Revelation* 22: 3-4, N.E.B.). God will give the grace of steady continuance, the grace if not 'to mount up with wings as eagles' or even 'to run and not be weary', at least 'to walk and not faint'. And perhaps that is the greatest grace of all.

Much hymnology has done great disservice to the interpretation of the clause 'Thy will be done in earth, as it is in heaven'. When I was a boy, I was often made to sing in Church Charlotte Elliott's hymn:

> 'My God, my Father, while I stray,
> Far from my home, on life's rough way,
> O teach me from my heart to say,
>   "Thy will be done".'

Now there is nothing exceptional about that. But the hymn was set to the gloomiest of tunes, and the refrain, according to the custom of the day, was marked '*p*' for *piano* – it had to be sung softly. The organist slowed down and often added a touch of sentimental *tremolo*. Then we went on, losing momentum as we went:

> 'What though in lonely grief I sigh
> For friends beloved no longer nigh,
> Submissive would I still reply,
>   "Thy Will be done".
>
> If Thou shouldst call me to resign
> What most I prize, it ne'er was mine;
> I only yield Thee what is Thine;
>   "Thy Will be done".'

And so on. When I grew up, I came to know and rejoice in Frederick Mann's invigorating hymn, set to an equally invigorating tune:

'My God, my Father, make me strong,
When tasks of life seem hard and long,
To greet them with this triumph song,
    Thy will be done.

Draw from my timid eyes the veil,
To show, where earthly forces fail,
Thy power and love must still prevail,
    Thy will be done.

With confident and humble mind,
Freedom in service I would find,
Praying through every toil assigned,
    Thy will be done.

Things deemed impossible I dare,
Thine is the call and thine the care,
Thy wisdom shall the way prepare,
    Thy will be done.

All power is here and round me now,
Faithful I stand in rule and vow,
While 'tis not I, but ever thou:
    Thy will be done.

Heaven's music chimes the glad days in,
Hope soars beyond death, pain, and sin,
Faith shouts in triumph, Love must win,
    Thy will be done.'

This prayer is not a moan, but a glad assent. It is the allying of my puny little will with the great and good will of Almighty Love made known to men in the person of Jesus Christ.

And when I so ally my will with His, I find that I am in good company. 'As it is (done) in heaven' – this is not elaborated or explained. It is a tantalising phrase, intended, presumably, to lift our eyes from the battlefield of the Church militant to the place where the heavenly hosts serve their Lord unhampered by the fetters of sin; where His servants worship Him and see Him face to face; where angels and archangels and all the company of heaven laud and magnify the glorious Name; where angelic ministrants are sent out to serve (*Hebrews* 1: 14).

'It is only quite recently I made that quotation ("with angels and archangels and all the company of heaven") a part of my private prayers – I festoon it round "hallowed be Thy name" ' (C. S. Lewis, *Letters to Malcolm Chiefly on Prayer*, p. 27). We may 'festoon' it round 'Thy will be done in earth, as it is in heaven'. It is wholly in place just there.

Give us this day our daily bread

So far the eyes of the disciple who prays this prayer have been turned Godwards. Prayer should always begin thus, in worship centred in God most holy, all loving, all powerful. It is not for us to rush into His presence with a list of our wants. Humble adoration, sincere alignment of our wills with His – this is where we begin. *Then* we may turn to petition. Jesus teaches us to ask for the simple basic things of life – food, forgiveness, guidance, deliverance from evil.

In these seven brief words there are several points of importance to note.

i. This is a prayer of *dependence*. It reminds us of our creatureliness – 'It is He that hath made us, and not we ourselves' (*Psalms* 100: 2, P.B.V.; 'and we are His', Revised Psalter). He who is our creator is also our sustainer. We depend on Him for each breath and for each day's food.

We need to pray this prayer, for the sin of hubris, of pride and of self-sufficiency, is a besetting one, especially to the men of a generation of great scientific achievement. 'Glory to Man in the highest, for Man is the master of things' – the lines of Swinburne are congenial to our modern outlook. Against that background, we must learn again the lesson of this clause of the Lord's prayer.

ii. 'Give *us* . . .' Who is *us*? We should give it the widest possible interpretation. We in the West are part of a world half of which is undernourished, a large part of which is on the edge of starvation. In this prayer, we align ourselves with our fellow-creatures in such a plight, and with God's concern for them. It is noteworthy that in this prayer, Jesus does not use the word *love* at all. But He does show an interest in people getting enough to eat. This is a word of wisdom for those who speak glibly about love and do little about meeting the immediate and urgent needs of their brothers and sisters.

iii. *Bread* for the belly. But man cannot live by bread alone. If it is true that he has a body which hungers for food, it is equally true that he has a mind which hungers for sustenance and a heart for love.

The world has been alerted, through the *Freedom from Hunger* campaign and other means, to the need to supply man's physical want. In this campaign the Church has played, and is playing, a significant part. Slowly but surely the Church is now awaking to the equally urgent need of supplying sustenance in the form of Christian literature for the awaking minds of newly literate millions. The United Nations Economic and Social Council Organisation has announced its intention of waging war on illiteracy. The World Council of Churches, at the end of 1963, pledged itself to raise a million pounds to see that Christian literature was made available for these hungry minds. Of this, the Church in Britain is responsible for about a quarter of a million pounds. The United Bible Societies, meeting in Tokyo at Whitsun 1963, determined to treble their circulation of Christian Scriptures by the end of 1966. All this is to the good – it is a sign of the awakening conscience of the Church. But it is only a tiny beginning. Against such efforts are reared the forces of atheistic Communism, of materialism, of pornography. The cause of Christian literature must be lifted from the bottom of the list of the Christian disciples' concerns to the top – and quickly, for we are engaged in a race against time.

Let this clause of the prayer be used, with persistence and urgency, as a prayer for the Christian Literature Movement.

iv. There is another, and a wider, sense in which this clause may be prayed. For the Christian, as for his Lord, his 'bread', his 'food', is the doing of the will of God. St. John, in a chapter remarkable for its vivid detail (ch. 4), tells of how the disciples, returning from a visit to the local Samaritan village, found Jesus greatly refreshed. When He arrived at the well, He had been hot and weary. Now, though they pressed Him to eat, He did not seem to need the food they brought Him. He explained: 'I have food to eat of which you know nothing ... It is meat and drink for me to do the will of Him who sent me until I have finished His work' (vv. 32, 34, N.E.B.).

Here, if we will but learn the lesson, is the deepest satisfaction of life – finding and fulfilling the will of God. Thus prayed, the clause means: 'Thy will be done in me this day. Thy kingdom come through me this day.' 'In His will is our peace', wrote St. Augustine. 'To do the will of Jesus, this is rest', wrote E. H. Bickersteth. 'I delight to do Thy will, O my God', wrote the Psalmist (*Psalms* 40: 8). This is food, bread, life.

v. 'Our *daily* bread.' The word (*epiousios*) is a very rare one;

indeed it occurs nowhere else in the New Testament except in this prayer. But it has turned up in the remains of a housekeeper's book found in Egypt, in the sense of the amount of daily food given to slaves, soldiers and labourers, and probably usually allotted a day beforehand. Hence Moffatt's rendering 'our bread for the morrow'. This suggests day-by-day trust in the providence of God. We do not ask for provision for the distant future, or for a blueprint of the way we should go in years ahead. God does not deal with us in that way. He leads us step by step, day by day; and as we trust in *that* way, we find Him adequate. So J. H. Newman wrote:

> 'Keep Thou my feet; I do not ask to see
> The distant scene; one step enough for me'.

One day at a time — this is the attitude of trust as it is also the antidote to worry. Several times, in this very chapter in which the Lord's prayer occurs, Jesus bids us 'put away anxious thoughts . . . do not ask anxiously . . . do not be anxious about tomorrow' (vv. 25, 31, 34, N.E.B.) — 'don't fash yourselves', as the Scots expressively have it. Worrying is the reverse of having faith. A child whose hand is firmly grasped in his father's does not worry.

Every Christian must work out for himself the tension between these two things: on the one hand, so to look and plan ahead, so to be 'provident', that he can move through life, and work through his programme, peacefully and purposefully; and on the other hand, so to live a day at a time as not to worry. 'Give us . . . our *daily* bread' — the future and its needs are in God's hands.

And forgive us our debts, as we forgive our debtors

To think of this as a kind of *quid pro quo* prayer — 'if we forgive those who wrong us, then forgiveness is our due' — is, of course, completely to misunderstand it. On any count, it is likely that I am guilty of worse sins than is my fellow-creature — a great plank is in my eye while he has a speck of sawdust in his (*St. Matthew* 7: 3, N.E.B.). We can never *earn* the divine forgiveness.

Rather, we have in this clause a principle laid down, a hard fact stated. If we refuse to forgive, then we so harden ourselves that the forgiveness of God cannot reach us. We grow an impenetrable callus of the soul. We hurt *ourselves* far more than we hurt the other man, as Saul hurt *himself* by kicking at the goad (*Acts* 26: 14, Moffatt). Men are made that way, as the gears of a car are made not to be forced. Force them, and you achieve nothing but a bad noise and a bad smell. (In some such way the second commandment must be understood. It is not the threat of a vengeful God who delights to visit fathers' sins on innocent children. It is simply the statement of a fact that the world is made in such a way that if we will insist on contravening its laws we must face the consequences – our species will be damaged.) So Jesus here states the fact that if we will not forgive one who has wronged us, we automatically shut ourselves off from the forgiveness of God. So important is the principle that this clause, alone of all the clauses of the prayer, has an explanatory addition in verses 14-15. And a long parable is devoted to its illustration (18: 23-35, and note also 5: 23-24).

This is the negative side of the teaching on forgiveness. The positive, creative side of forgiveness can be seen worked out in the life and example of Jesus and indeed of His followers all down the ages. 'Father, forgive them . . .', He prayed for His murderers. 'Lord, do not hold this sin against them', Stephen prayed in the same fashion for his murderers. 'If Stephen had not prayed, the Church would not have had Paul', St. Augustine argued (Sermon 315). We may add: 'If Stephen had not *forgiven* . . .' Each succeeding century provides its examples of the healing, creative power of forgiveness.

But another problem is involved, at least by implication, in this clause. If it is a question of A sinning against me, the teaching, though searching and solemn, is clear. But suppose A sins against B, my brother in Christ, and I am conscious of a gross perversion of what is right – what then? What do I do, smarting under the sense of a deep wrong done to a fellow-Christian? Certain things are clear. I continue to love A. I continue to hold A in my prayers. And it may be that I shall rebuke A. It may be – but here I shall be on my guard, for rebuke may involve anger, and wholly righteous anger is a rare thing. Temper, animosity, all too easily enter into it. That is why St. Paul warns us that anger is a bad bed-companion – 'Be angry', he writes – anger *can* be good, a sinew of the soul. 'Be angry, but do not sin. Do not let the sun go down on your wrath. That would be to give the devil his chance' (*Ephesians* 4: 26-27; cf. St. James 1: 19-20, Moffatt, 'slow to be angry – for human anger does not promote divine righteousness'). But when I can be reasonably sure that my anger 'is the fluid love bleeds when you cut it' (C. S. Lewis), then I may direct it against one who can clearly be seen to have wronged a brother in Christ.

Beneath the Cross made of two charred beams in the ruins of Coventry Cathedral are inscribed the two words 'Father, forgive'.

Not three words, 'Father, forgive *them*', but two. For we all of us have a share in the sin of the world and in its shame. We all of us need the forgiveness of God. 'Forgive *us* our trespasses.'

And lead us not into temptation,
  but deliver us from (the) evil (one)

The wording of the first half of this petition has caused difficulty for many, a difficulty but little eased by the rendering 'Let us not be led into temptation'. Naturally, we do not like to think of God tempting men. We recall the words of St. James (1: 13): 'Let no man say when he is tempted, I am tempted of God: for God . . . tempteth no man'.

· The petition is best understood as an admission of our frailty, an acknowledgement of our liability to sin. Suddenly, unexpectedly, when we are off our guard, when we are over-strained or tired, temptation strikes and we are down! The language of the Prayer Book collects is interesting at this point. Let it be granted that 'all assaults of our enemies', 'the power of any adversaries', 'any kind of danger', 'the fear of our enemies', 'all perils and dangers of this night', may have originally referred to physical dangers of robbers or unlit streets and 'things that go bump in the night'. But they surely also refer to the assaults of the evil one into which we fall so easily. 'Seeing, brethren, that we are weak men, but entrusted with a great office' – so Bishop Ridding rightly warns the clergy at the beginning of his *Litany of Remembrance*.

John Baillie, in one of his addresses in *Christian Devotion* (pp. 33-34), has some wise words on temptation:

'The devil is indeed a past master in the art of the surprise attack. So subtle is he in his approach, so alluring are the forms and the dresses which he can assume, that there is little chance for us unless we are actively on the look-out for him. "Whenever I am about to commit any folly", says Bucklaw in Scott's *Bride of Lammermuir*, "he persuades me it is the most necessary, gallant gentleman-like thing on earth, and I am up to saddle-girths in the bog before I see that the ground is soft." Our only chance of escape lies in' preparedness, and in the discourse of Jesus this preparedness is always connected with prayer. "Watch and pray", He repeats. And St. Paul repeats it too. "Continue in prayer, and watch in the same." Prayer is *the soul's vigil*. It is the most effective of all vigils. The devil has never such difficulty with us as when he finds us on our knees. Even then, it is true, he will not altogether own defeat. When we are praying for protection against one sin, he can make us commit another; but it is very difficult indeed for him to make us commit the very sin against which we are praying. Hence the better we understand what our besetting sins are, and the more diligently and particularly we pray for grace to overcome them, the safer we shall be. It was said that the Battle of Waterloo was really won, not on a plain in Brabant, but on the playing-fields of Eton. So it is that sin is conquered—not in the moment of temptation but in the long prayerful discipline that precedes it. And our Lord's warning is that unless we thus arm ourselves in advance, we shall find, when the temptation comes, that it is now too late. "Sleep on now, and take your rest . . . the hour is come"; what more tragic words than these have ever been spoken?

It would be wrong, then, to be misled by those who are now so ready with the opposite advice, telling us that the best way to deal with sin is never to think about it, and that it will be time enough to cross our bridges when we come to them. Rather listen to the following, "Keep the faculty of effort alive in you by a little gratuitous exercise every day. That is, be systematically ascetic or heroic in little unnecessary points, do every day or two something for no other reason than that you would rather not do it, so that when the hour of dire need draws nigh, it may find you not unnerved to stand the test." From what first-century apocalypse do you think that comes? Or from what Puritan directory? It is from William James's very modern textbook of psychology.'

We frustrate the answering of this prayer when, inviting the situation in which it is easy to sin, we virtually step into temptation. The obvious illustration is the gloating over an unclean book or the harbouring in our minds of an unclean picture. But, more subtly, we allow such a situation to arise when, *unnecessarily*, we lapse into bad health or extremes of tiredness, or when, refusing relaxation, we forget our call to be God's athletes. On such occasions we lead ourselves into temptation, and it is of little avail to ask God not to lead us!

The petition calls for two other comments:

i. For all that we have just said, there is a sense in which the Bible speaks of God tempting His children. He tests them, and in the testing He refines and strengthens them. 'It came to pass . . . that God did *prove* Abraham' (*Genesis* 22: 1, R.V.). 'Whence shall we buy bread, that these may eat?' Jesus asks Philip. 'And this', comments the evangelist, significantly, 'this He said to *prove* him' (*St. John* 6: 5-6). In both these instances the verb is that from which the noun 'temptation' in this petition is derived. So God makes muscles for His servants. Have we not all known Christians whose characters have been strengthened and beautified almost beyond recognition by the fires of testing? 'When He hath tried me, I shall come forth as gold' (*Job* 23: 10).

It is this kind of thing that St. James was thinking of when he wrote: 'Count it all joy when ye fall into divers temptations; knowing this, that the trying of your faith worketh patience' (1: 2-3 — 'such testing of your faith breeds fortitude', N.E.B.). And Robert Browning:

> 'Then, welcome each rebuff
> That turns earth's smoothness rough,
> Each sting that bids nor sit nor stand but go!'
> (*Rabbi ben Ezra*, vi)

ii. Professor Jeremias thinks that this phrase may have an eschatological connotation — 'preserve us from falling away in the last temptation, when the secrets of evil will be revealed'. Certainly the clauses 'Hallowed be Thy name' and 'Thy kingdom come' both have an eschatological reference; they quote the old Jewish prayer, the *Qaddish*, imploring God to reveal His final glory, asking for the coming of the hour in which God's name will be hallowed for ever and His kingdom prevail. The petitions for bread and for forgiveness are for the here and now — this is 'realised eschatology', the message that God's kingdom is already effective if men open their hearts. Then in the last clause we swing back to the fully eschatological note — 'preserve us from falling away in the last temptation'. This would certainly be in keeping with the strong eschatological note which recurs throughout St. Matthew's Gospel (for example, at the end of all of his five 'books' of the teaching of Jesus — 7: 21 ff.; 10: 40 ff.; 13: 47 ff.; 18: 23 ff.; 24, 25).

'But deliver us from evil' — the original does not make it clear whether the adjective is neuter ('what is evil') or whether it is masculine ('the evil one', Satan, evil 'personified'). We cannot tell which idea was in the mind of our Lord — or whether, perhaps, both ideas were. What is clear is that the negative of the first half of the petition ('lead us not . . .') gives place to the urgent, positive plea of the second ('deliver us').

What is equally clear is that it was the experience of the members of the early Church — as it has been that of their descendants down the years — that in Christ this prayer was abundantly answered. There is a lyrical note about the words of the writer of the Epistle to the Colossians: God 'has *delivered us* from the dominion of darkness and transferred us to the kingdom of His beloved Son'

(1: 13, R.S.V.). The language is similar to that of the prayer There has, as it were, been a change of sphere. The sphere in which evil, the power of darkness. held sway has been exchanged for the sphere in which God's beloved Son reigns in power. The kingdom has arrived with His coming, His cross, and His resurrection. The powers of the Age to come have invaded this Age — and we are delivered from (the) evil (one).

So Pascal could write: 'And so I hold out my arms to my Liberator, who ... came to suffer and to die for me on the earth ... And by His grace I await death in peace, in the hope of being eternally united to Him; and yet I live with joy, either in the prosperity that it pleases Him to give me, or in the ills that He may send for my good, and which He has taught me to endure after His example.' That is the true spirit of this clause of the Lord's Prayer.

For thine is the kingdom, and the power, and the glory, for ever

This doxology, absent from the original text of the Gospel, is found in the *Didache*, the earliest existing Christian Church-order, which some date early in the second century. Its absence 'does not mean that Jesus intended his prayer to be recited without a word of praise at the end. But in the very earliest times, the doxology had no fixed form, and its precise wording was left to those who prayed. Later on, when the Lord's Prayer began to be used in the services of the Church as a common prayer, it was felt necessary to establish the doxology in a fixed form' (J. Jeremias).

So much for the textual and liturgical background of these words. Now for their interpretation.

They are a statement of fact uttered in faith. Though now we see not all things put under Him, yet His *is* the kingdom and the power and the glory. The cross and resurrection of Jesus are to us the assurance that we shall see the final triumph of right over wrong, of light over darkness. The kingdom, ushered in with the incarnation of our Lord, will reach its full and perfect consummation at His coming. He must reign. The power is in the hands of almighty Love. The glory will be His alone.

But the words are more than a statement of fact. They are a paean of praise. We shall notice that St. Paul delights to end his prayers with praise (e.g. *Ephesians* 3: 20-21). As some of his great dogmatic passages burgeon out into praise (e.g. *Romans* 11: 33-36 — R. H. Strachan said that 'his dogmas are all doxologies'), so do his prayers. So does this Lord's Prayer. This is not only a good liturgical principle. It is good theology and it is good religion. It is an expression of true religious experience, that right prayer issues in adoration and thanksgiving and praise.

Consider what he has done who has prayed this prayer. He has looked up into the face of God and called him 'Father'. Now a father, if he is worthy of that title, wills nothing but good for his child. If that is true on the human level, how much truer it is of God in His relationship to His children! The man who prays the opening clause of this prayer acknowledges that true blessedness is to be found only when we rest in the fact that 'in His will is our peace'. The Christian, therefore, is the integrated, the fundamentally happy man, because he is 'in the will of God', at peace. He does not fret. To use the ugly but eloquent modern colloquialism, he does not 'flap'. He lives as one whose Father is the Most High. The so-called Sermon on the Mount begins with a description of the Christian disciple (*St. Matthew* 5: 1 ff.). If the opening verses were translated back into the Aramaic in which they were originally spoken, they would be seen to be a series of exclamations – 'O how happy are the poor! . . . O how happy are they that mourn! . . .' Indeed, the New English Bible gives these verses their proper exclamatory form – 'How blest . . . ! How blest . . . !'

Naturally, then, the man who prays this prayer finds himself engaging frequently in adoration – in the Doxology, or in the *Gloria*, or in some other kind of thanksgiving. He can hardly do otherwise. He does not shut his eyes to the evil in the world – sin and suffering and death are realities to him. He does not expect to escape them just because he is a son of God. They come at him as they come at others – he is not exempt from 'the slings and arrows of outrageous fortune'. But he can 'give thanks always *for all things*' (*Ephesians* 5: 20) because he is in touch with a God who has a way of turning life's minuses into pluses, life's negatives into positives, life's minor keys into triumphant majors. He turned the cross into a sign of victory, so that Christ reigned from the tree. He has been doing this kind of thing ever since. So the disciple begins to understand what St. Paul meant when he wrote 'All things are yours' – and included death in the list! (1 *Corinthians* 3: 21-22). Death is yours, for you are Christ's and Christ is God's – so the ogre becomes a friend, and what unregenerate man regards as the final full-stop becomes the entrance into life abundant and eternal.

We shall see this in the life and prayers of our Lord, and of St.

Paul. We shall see it in that most grim book of the New Testament, the Revelation of St. John, which is shot through with songs of triumph – the shout breaks through the noise of battle because the victory is assured.

We can see this in the lives of the saints. Listen to William Law: 'Would you know who is the greatest saint in the world? It is not he who prays most, it is not he who gives most alms, or is most eminent for temperance, chastity, or justice. But it is he who is most thankful to God, and who has a heart always ready to praise God. This is the perfection of all virtues. Joy in God and thankfulness to God is the highest perfection of a divine and holy life.' And he adds: 'To thank God only for such things as you like is no more a proper act of piety than to believe only what you see is an act of faith'.

Listen to William Grimshaw of Haworth, fulfilling his long ministry in a dour part of the Yorkshire moors. He prays: 'Though I dare not say I will never repine, yet I hope I may say, I will labour not only to submit, but to acquiesce; not only to bear Thy heaviest afflictions on me, but to consent to them, and *praise Thee for them*' (G. G. Cragg, *Grimshaw of Haworth*, p. 117).

Thanksgiving rises into adoration when we learn to say, as the Jews in their liturgy constantly said, *baruch Adonai*, 'blessed (is or be) the Lord!' 'The Old Testament furnishes plenty of stately examples of liturgies of adoration based upon this phrase, shot through with this attitude of adoration of God for His own sake, for His being, for His creation, and for His mighty works, as well as, in particular, for His work of rescuing His people . . . This attitude of "benediction" is at the heart . . . of Jewish worship' (C. F. D. Moule, *The Birth of the New Testament*, pp. 19-20). And adoration, as William Temple reminded us, is 'the most selfless emotion of which our nature is capable and therefore the chief remedy for that self-centredness which is our original sin and the source of all actual sin' (*Readings in St. John's Gospel*, p. 68).

So the Prayer reaches its climax in words of adoration. It has taught us to think of God as *Father* ('Our Father'), as *King* ('Thy kingdom come'), as *Governor* ('Thy will be done'), as *Provider* ('Give us . . . bread'), as *Pardoner* ('Forgive us our trespasses'), as *Guide* ('Lead us . . .'), as *Deliverer* ('Deliver us from evil'). The prayer which began with the adoration of God and proceeded to petition swings back to the God-centred attitude of adoration in the Doxology – 'Thine is the kingdom, and the power, and the glory, for ever.'

Amen

This is one of the most abused words in our Christian vocabulary. We regard it as little more than a full-stop to a prayer. We accord it but little meaning. We use it as a mere breathing-space in which we can ask ourselves: 'What comes next in the liturgical *menu?*'

But *Amen* is a great word, strong and powerful. It is a word of asseveration. It puts into two brief syllables the meditative gladness of a great assent – '*so be it!*'

Sometimes it should be shouted – how wonderful to have a share in the divine plan, in God's strategy for His world and His Church! 'Amen; so be it! By His mercy, He and I are in on this together!'

Sometimes it should be deliberately whispered. The way of the cross is costly. It will hurt. But 'Amen; so be it! He calls. I follow – even unto death'. *Amen* is assent, and assent involves sacrifice.

The biographer of Studdert Kennedy, in trying to assess his attitude to prayer, writes: 'True prayer, when it is that kind which asks, is for courage to endure, never for permission to survive' (William Purcell, *Woodbine Willie*, p. 148). *That* is to say *Amen* from a full heart.

'It is finished' was our Lord's *Amen* to the Father's will. He who was the *Amen* thus said His *Amen* – 'Finished! Fulfilled!' (cf. *St. John* 19: 30; and see pp. 73 ff.).

St. Matthew 11: 25-26

A.V.	N.E.B.
25. I thank thee, O Father, Lord of heaven and earth, because thou hast hid these things from the wise and prudent, and hast revealed them unto babes.	'I thank thee, Father, Lord of heaven and earth, for hiding these things from the learned and wise, and revealing them to the simple.
26. Even so, Father: for so it seemed good in thy sight.	Yes, Father, such was thy choice.'

The parallel passage in St. Luke runs:

St. Luke 10: 21

A.V.	N.E.B.
21. I thank thee, O Father, Lord of heaven and earth, that thou hast hid these things from the wise and prudent, and hast revealed them unto babes: even so, Father; for so it seemed good in thy sight.	'I thank thee, Father, Lord of heaven and earth, for hiding these things from the learned and wise, and revealing them to the simple. Yes, Father, such was thy choice.'

The setting in which this prayer occurs in St. Matthew is worthy of note. The evangelist prefaces it with two incidents:

i. vv. 2-19 – the story of the mission of St. John the Baptist's disciples to our Lord and His tribute to His forerunner. Jesus drew their attention – and ours – to one who was utterly unsophisticated, self-effacing, devoted to his appointed task of preparing a way for the Messiah. Blunt and outspoken to a degree, he lacked those qualities which the world associates with 'the wise and prudent'. But Jesus said of him that 'among them that are born of women there hath not risen a greater . . .' (v. 11).

ii. vv. 20-24 – the story of our Lord's utterance of woes upon the cities where He had done most of His mighty works. Perhaps then, as sometimes now, the men of culture and education who lived in the cities looked down on the 'rustics', the 'babes' who were their country neighbours. But privilege did not of itself bring insight. These, the 'wise and prudent' of their day, did not repent though they had Jesus in their midst. They rejected Him.

St. Luke prefaces the prayer first with the story of the woes uttered upon the cities which had spurned our Lord (10: 10-16), and secondly with the story of the return of the seventy disciples from their evangelistic expedition (vv. 17-20). Their mission had been attended by great success; God's reign was proving victorious over the powers of evil; Satan was falling from heaven like a flash of lightning out of the sky. How wonderfully God had worked through 'men whom worldlings count as fools'! Jesus turned to prayer, and thanked His Father that such was His choice (v. 21, N.E.B.).

Returning to St. Matthew, we note that the verses in which this prayer occurs (vv. 25-30) consist *first*, of the prayer itself (vv. 25-26); *secondly*, of a meditation on the relationship of the Son to the Father, prayer gliding into meditation, thanksgiving and meditation being intertwined (v. 27); and *thirdly*, of the invitation of our Lord to 'come . . . take My yoke . . . learn of Me', and the promise of rest under His yoke (vv. 28-30). We are here concerned with the first of these sections.

Twice in these two verses, our Lord addresses God as 'Father'. It was His habitual form of address (see pp. 19 ff.). To this, in the first instance, is added the phrase 'Lord of heaven and earth'. Just as, in the Lord's Prayer, 'Father' is qualified by 'which art in heaven', so here 'Father' is qualified by 'Lord of heaven and earth'. Thus once again we see a union of intimacy and majesty in the form of address (see pp. 21 ff.).

Now we may picture the Master surrounded by the Twelve. It could be said of them in all truth, as it was to be said of the Corinthians by St. Paul a few years later, that 'not many wise men after the flesh, not many mighty, not many noble' had been called (1 *Corinthians* 1 · 26). There must have been times when Jesus was tempted to despair of them. There were times when He rebuked them for their unbelief (*St. Matthew* 8: 26; 16: 8, etc.) and for their slowness in understanding who He was (*St. John* 14: 9). But in this passage, as our Lord turned His heart and mind to God, He did not complain of their lack of perception, of their obtuseness, or of their lack of education and distinction. He thanked God that He had hidden these things from the learned and wise and revealed them to the simple.

What is the meaning of this? It is a reminder of the fact that there is no intellectual favouritism with God. The road to God is not the Gnostic road, a road for the intellectual élite alone. There are illiterate children of God who know more of Him than do some graduates in theology, as some missionaries have found to their surprise when they have first gone abroad, and some curates have found when they have gone from theological college to their first parish. This is not to say that God puts a premium on ignorance; far from it. In the New Testament, childlikeness is never confused with childishness — 'do not be childish, my friends', wrote St. Paul to the Corinthians. 'Be as innocent of evil as babes, but at least be grown-up in your thinking' (1 *Corinthians* 14: 20, N.E.B.). It is a primary obligation of the Christian religion to 'love the Lord thy God with all thy . . . mind'. But it *is* to assert that lack of intellectual or educational privilege in itself need be no barrier between a man and his God. Intellectual achievement has been known to throw up a barrier of pride. St. Paul has some words of stern wisdom for the man 'who fancies himself wise' (1 *Corinthians* 3: 18, N.E.B.).

Only when a man is lowly enough to become a little child can he enter the Kingdom of heaven (*St. Mark* 10: 15). The fact that Jesus was surrounded by what His contemporaries thought to be the riff-raff of society, tax-gatherers and sinners, blind and lame, and that the children sang to Him, scandalised the religious leaders of the day, but rejoiced His heart (*St. Matthew* 21: 14-17).

When Frederick Denison Maurice, on his ordination in 1834, went to a very small parish of about 250 souls in Warwickshire, he described his parishioners as 'a set of farmers and labourers, most of whom have not a notion beyond their traces'. Writing to Acland (afterwards Sir T. Acland) of people who misunderstood him, he said: 'Nobody sees what I mean, and I return humbled if not dejected into myself, half convinced that I have no business with any but my own little flock, who may, I hope, by God's grace, be taught to *feel* what a catholic Church is, though they may never *understand* the name'. (The italics are mine; the distinction is worth noting. The letter is quoted in *Toward the Recovery of Unity: The Thought of Frederick Denison Maurice*, edited from his Letters . . . by John F. Porter and William J. Wolf, p. 65.)

St. Matthew 26: 39, 42

A.V.	N.E.B.
39. O my Father, if it be possible, let this cup pass from me: nevertheless not as I will, but as thou wilt.	'My Father, if it is possible, let this cup pass me by. Yet not as I will, but as thou wilt.'
42. O my Father, if this cup may not pass away from me, except I drink it, thy will be done.	'My Father, if it is not possible for this cup to pass me by without my drinking it, thy will be done.'

The parallel passage in St. Mark runs:

St. Mark 14: 36

A.V.	N.E.B.
36. Abba, Father, all things are possible unto thee; take away this cup from me: nevertheless not what I will, but what thou wilt.	'Abba, Father, all things are possible to thee; take this cup away from me. Yet not what I will, but what thou wilt.'

And in St. Luke:

St. Luke 22: 42

A.V.	N.E.B.
42. Father, if thou be willing, remove this cup from me: nevertheless not my will, but thine, be done.	'Father, if it be thy will, take this cup away from me. Yet not my will but thine be done.'

That the prayer for the passing of the cup and the doing of the Father's will was thrice repeated is clearly stated by St. Matthew (v. 44), but not quite so explicitly by St. Mark, where the interest is focused more on Peter and his companions and their failure to watch at the hour of crisis. St. Luke does not stress the repetition of the prayer, but gives details about our Lord's distress and about His sweat of blood which are lacking in the other accounts.

In St. Matthew's account our Lord addresses God as 'My Father'. He does not now pray 'Our Father', for this is not a family prayer. Here He is having dealings with God which He alone can have. Here is lonely encounter. St. Luke records the address as simply 'Father', St. Mark as 'Abba' and adds the translation from Aramaic into Greek. (On 'Abba' see pp. 20-21.)

The 'cup' is in the Old Testament very frequently used as a metaphor of the judgement of God (e.g. *Psalms* 11: 6; 75: 8) and of His wrath (*Isaiah* 51: 17; *Jeremiah* 25: 15). The metaphor is here used because the cross was to be the place where the love of God, coming into contact with the sin of the world borne by the Son of God, burst into flame.

It has frequently been pointed out that many a martyr, Socrates included, went to his death with less apparent foreboding, less shrinking, less 'anguish of spirit' (*St. Luke* 22: 44, N.E.B.) than did our Lord to His. The question has been asked 'Why?' At least two considerations must be borne in mind:

i. *The true humanity of Jesus.* Most Christians pay lip-service to this doctrine, but many are at heart docetists – they really believe in a God who assumed the *appearance* of humanity but not the real thing. Such need to ponder again the figure of the Christ of Gethsemane, and to read the commentary on that episode in His life which the author of the Epistle to the Hebrews gives in chapter 5: 7-9 – 'In the days of His earthly life He offered up prayers and petitions, with loud cries and tears, to God who was able to deliver Him from the grave. Because of His humble submission His prayer was heard: son though He was, He learned obedience in the school of suffering, and, once perfected, became the source of eternal salvation for all who obey Him . . .' (N.E.B.).

C. S. Lewis, in his *Letters to Malcolm* (especially pp. 62 and 85) makes much of the Gethsemane incident, which he regards as the beginning of the Passion. He points out that our Lord had long foreseen His death, an inevitable consequence of conduct such as His in a world such as ours. But he holds that this knowledge must have been withdrawn from Him in Gethsemane, for He 'could not . . . have prayed that the cup might pass and simultaneously known that it would not'. This means that, at the last moment, there were loosed on Him precisely those torments which afflict us – the torments of hope (had not Isaac been spared at the last moment?) and of suspense and of anxiety. He 'was in *all* points tempted like as we are, yet without sin' (*Hebrews* 4: 15).

ii. *The mystery of godlessness.* Death by crucifixion was an ordeal of the most horrible kind. Jesus must have seen others die who had been condemned to it. No wonder He shrank from it! But there is more than physical revulsion behind the thrice-repeated cry. In some way which the human mind can never fully fathom, Jesus was to take upon Himself the load of human sin and folly. This it was which made the prospect of death well-nigh intolerable, as it was this which wrung from Him the cry: 'My God, My God, why hast Thou forsaken Me?'

But He triumphed. He broke through the shrinking and the quivering. He learnt obedience through the things which He suffered. He uttered His great assent: 'Nevertheless, not as I will, but as Thou wilt' (v. 39); 'Thy will be done' (v. 42). So at the hour of greatest crisis, He lived out the lesson which He had learnt at His mother's knee, the lesson *she* learnt when at her hour of crisis she said: 'Behold the handmaid of the Lord; be it unto me according to Thy word' (*St. Luke* 1: 38; see pp. 26-27 and 48-49).

The prayer in Gethsemane did not preserve His body from crucifixion. But it helped to preserve His utter obedience to the Father – and that was what mattered.

St. Matthew 27: 46

A.V.	N.E.B.
46. And about the ninth hour Jesus cried with a loud voice, saying, Eli, Eli, lama sabachthani? that is to say, My God, my God, why hast thou forsaken me?	And about three Jesus cried aloud, '*Eli, Eli, lema sabachthani?*', which means, 'My God, my God, why hast thou forsaken me?'

The parallel passage in St. Mark runs:

St. Mark 15: 34

A.V.	N.E.B.
34. And at the ninth hour Jesus cried with a loud voice, saying, Eloi, Eloi, lama sabachthani? which is, being interpreted, My God, my God, why hast thou forsaken me?	And at three Jesus cried aloud, '*Eli, Eli, lema sabachthani?*', which means, 'My God, my God, why hast thou forsaken me?'

Of the seven words uttered by our Lord on the cross and recorded in the four Gospels, this is the only one in St. Matthew and in St. Mark. Two of the words are not prayers ('Woman, behold thy son' . . . 'Son, behold thy mother', and 'Verily, verily, I say unto thee, today thou shalt be with Me in paradise'). 'I thirst' (*St. John* 19: 28) and 'It is finished' (*St. John* 19: 30) may be called prayers, for reasons which will be made clear when we come to consider them under the prayers in the Fourth Gospel.

The first thing to note about this cry from the cross is that it is a quotation from *Psalms* 22: 1. Both St. Matthew and St. Mark give it in the Aramaic form in which Jesus would naturally have spoken. It is highly significant that, in His hour of direct suffering, as in the hour of His fierce temptation (*St. Matthew* 4: 1-11), His mind should have been so saturated with His Scriptures that they should have sprung to His lips. We shall notice this again when we come to consider *St. Luke* 23: 46, 'Father, into Thy hands I commend my spirit', for that cry is also a quotation. The writer of Psalm 22 was most probably expressing not merely his own grief but the grief of his people. It is likely that Jesus, in repeating this bitter cry, was identifying Himself with the age-old agony of the Jewish people, of whom, according to the flesh, He was one. Thus the ministry, which began with an act of identification with His people at His baptism, ended with another act of identification.

This prayer of dereliction should be read in close conjunction with the prayer for the removal of the cup recorded by all three Synoptists (*St. Matthew* 26: 39, 42; see pp. 44 ff.). What was written there about the true humanity of Jesus and about the mystery of godlessness applies in even greater measure to this cry at the crucifixion than it did to the prayer which was the prelude to the passion. It should be pondered over again.

From the darkness of those hours (v. 45) and from that cry of dereliction, we see not only the awfulness of the sin of the individual and of the sin of the world, but also the love of a holy God who grapples with it. 'It is the holiness of God that calls for the work of Christ *and provides it*' (P. T. Forsyth). 'God was in Christ, reconciling the world unto Himself' (2 *Corinthians* 5: 19).

ST. LUKE

St. Luke 1: 38

A.V.	N.E.B.
38. And Mary said, Behold the handmaid of the Lord; be it unto me according to thy word.	'Here am I,' said Mary; 'I am the Lord's servant; as you have spoken, so be it.'

THIS, though addressed, strictly speaking, to the angel-messenger, is in fact a prayer to God. It is a prayer of consent. It is the Blessed Virgin Mary's great assent to the divine will. It is her whole-hearted 'Yes' to the mind of God as it has just been disclosed to her. *His* will shall be *her* will. She will be His – to bear (in more senses than one), to offer, to suffer. In the working out of this assent in the coming years a sword would pierce her soul, as the nails were to pierce her Son's body. There would be much to puzzle her ('Son, *why* hast thou thus dealt with us?' (*St. Luke* 2: 48; and note also *St. Matthew* 12: 46-50). But, as at the very beginning there had been a great assent, albeit a trembling one, so at the end also there would be her assent, and she would be found at the foot of the cross, when most of the others had fled (*St. John* 19: 25).

'The handmaid of the Lord.' The New English Bible translates it 'the Lord's servant'. It is simply the feminine form of the word which so frequently occurs in the New Testament and is translated servant or slave. We have already seen the probable influence of this attitude on the part of the Blessed Virgin Mary on her Son – both in teaching Him to pray the great prayer of assent ('Thy will be done') and in interpreting His ministry of Messiahship in terms of the Servant of the Lord (see pp. 26 ff.).

So we watch Mother and Son at prayer, and in doing so we tread on holy ground. Evelyn Underhill tells this story: 'A traveller who had paid her first visit to Iona was asked by an old Highland gardener where she had been. When she told him, he said, "Ay! Iona iss a very thin place". She asked him what he meant and he replied, "There's no much between Iona and the Lord" ' (*Collected Papers*, p. 196).

The man who stays awhile in *this* place, pondering on Mother and Son at their prayers, may well find this also to be 'a very thin place'.

St. Luke 2: 29-32

A.V.	N.E.B.
29. Lord, now lettest thou thy servant depart in peace, according to thy word:	'This day, Master, thou givest thy servant his discharge in peace; now thy promise is fulfilled.
30. For mine eyes have seen thy salvation,	For I have seen with my own eyes the deliverance
31. Which thou hast prepared before the face of all people;	Which thou hast made ready in full view of all the nations:
32. A light to lighten the Gentiles, and the glory of thy people Israel.	A light that will be a revelation to the heathen, and glory to thy people Israel.'

The *Nunc Dimittis* is a prayer in a sense in which the *Magnificat* (1: 46 ff.) and the *Benedictus* (1: 68 ff.) are not. (The *Magnificat* is a Psalm of exultation, based on that of Hannah in 1 *Samuel* 2: 1-10; and the *Benedictus*, which is styled 'prophecy', is in part addressed to the infant John, later to be called the Baptist. Hence their exclusion from this book. The *Nunc Dimittis*, being prayer pure and simple, is included.)

Let us recapture the scene behind St. Luke's introduction to the *Nunc Dimittis* (vv. 25-28). The voice of prophecy had long been silent in Israel. The Messianic hope had sometimes almost died out, sometimes flared up fiercely, centred on some self-styled deliverer. But in the hearts of a few of the faithful it had burned on quietly with a steady glow. Hope deferred had sometimes made the heart sick; but there were always those who 'watched and waited for the restoration of Israel' (v. 25, N.E.B.), sure that the Messiah would come, and that meanwhile it was their calling to bear the witness of an upright and devout life. Simeon was one of these, a man on whom the Holy Spirit could rest, a man accustomed to be guided by that Spirit (vv. 25, 27). He was indeed a *servant* of the Lord (v. 29 – the word is the same as that which, in its feminine form, is used in 1: 38).

Now the evening of his life has come. His days of service are over, and he can receive his Master's discharge (v. 29, N.E.B.). It is a picture of perfect peace and of hope fulfilled, as the old man takes the tiny Babe in his arms.

49

There are several points worthy of note here:

i. God may tarry long beyond the time we hope for, but He never breaks His word. His promise is always fulfilled (v. 29). So Simeon proved, and so the saints have proved down the ages. Together with faith and love, hope occupies a place of honour among the New Testament virtues. Christian hope is based on the faithfulness of God Who is Himself the *Amen*, the utterly reliable, the faithful and true.

ii. As the old man looks at the little Child, he describes Him as God's 'deliverance' (v. 31, N.E.B.). Christianity is more than enlightenment. It *is* that, and Simeon, in the next verse, speaks in terms of 'a light that will be a revelation . . . and glory . . .' But it is also a divine rescue operation directed to man in his need – that above all else. Had not the angel-messenger told Joseph that the Child's name should be called Jesus, 'for it is He who will save His people from their sins' (*St. Matthew* 1 : 21, Phillips)?

What did the phrase mean to Simeon? Was he thinking in terms of rescue from the cruelty of a Roman yoke, of the restoration of Israel's political sovereignty for which he had watched and waited so long? No doubt he was. But those shrewd old eyes, keen with the clarity of holiness, saw more than that. Israel needed something deeper than a political deliverance on nationalistic lines. Israel needed to regain the liberty of the sons of God. This it was which the Child would make possible.

iii. The scope of the efficacy of this 'deliverance' is thought of in terms of the world ('the nations,' v. 31, 'the heathen,' v. 32, N.E.B.) and of God's own people Israel. From Israel the glory had departed; in Christ it would be restored.

Readers of Dr. Kenneth Scott Latourette's works will be familiar with his picture of the advancing waves of Christian missionary endeavour, and especially of his description of the two great bursts of Western missionary activity in the fifteenth to the seventeenth centuries and from the end of the eighteenth century. The result is that in practically every country of the world the Christian Church exists. Sometimes its roots are planted firmly, sometimes in soil all too shallow. But the light of revelation has shone 'in full view of all the nations', and God's salvation has been seen.

St. Luke 22: 31-32

A.V.	N.E.B.
31. And the Lord said, Simon, Simon, behold, Satan hath desired to have you, that he may sift you as wheat:	'Simon, Simon, take heed: Satan has been given leave to sift all of you like wheat;
32. But I have prayed for thee, that thy faith fail not: and when thou art converted, strengthen thy brethren.	But for you I have prayed that your faith may not fail; and when you have come to yourself, you must lend strength to your brothers.'

The setting of this prayer is a sordid one. The disciples, almost under the shadow of the coming crucifixion, have been discussing which of them was the greatest. No wonder that the discussion elicited a rebuke from the Master (vv. 24-27). But the sordid discussion and the rebuke were relieved by (*a*) His tribute to their continuing with Him in His times of testing (v. 28), and (*b*) His promise to them of a kingdom and of places near Him when that kingdom came (vv. 29-30).

Then comes a most searching passage. The Lord addresses Peter by his old name, Simon — a reminder, perhaps, of his frailty before Christ took him in hand with the promise that he would become the Rock-man. The reminder is made the more forceful by the repetition of the name. Jesus refers to the grave spiritual dangers through which *all* the disciples have been passing ('you' in v. 31 is plural), and adds 'but I have made supplication for *thee*, that thy faith fail not'. This passing from the group to the individual is most impressive. Christ must have seen at once the weakness of Simon Peter and the possibilities for good and for leadership latent within him. Hence the concentration of His prayers on him.

In the Ordination Addresses of Bishop J. B. Lightfoot occur these words: 'The touch of Christ, the voice of Christ, the look of Christ, but above all the prayer of Christ! "I have prayed for thee". What else shall we need if only we realise this! Christ interceding for me, *Christ concentrating His prayer on me*, Christ individualising His merits for me . . . !' (p. 135). The italics are mine, but the words thus italicised suggest that what the Lord did for Peter in the days of His flesh He still does for other frail folk like us. If He could make a man of sterling character and eventually a martyr out

of the uncertain stuff of which Simon was made, who is to say that
His prayers will not avail even for us? The heavenly intercession of
Christ continues now and throughout time for His whole Church
and, we may dare to believe, for the individual members of it. The
writer of the Epistle to the Hebrews expounds this with great care,
insisting that the true manhood of Christ is the guarantee of His
perfect understanding of us (4: 14-16).

> 'Where high the heavenly temple stands,
> The house of God not made with hands,
> A great High Priest our nature wears,
> The Guardian of mankind appears.
>
> Our fellow-sufferer yet retains
> A fellow-feeling of our pains,
> And still remembers in the skies
> His tears, his agonies, and cries.'
>
> (*Michael Bruce*)

Several other points about this prayer call for comment.

i. In v. 31, the Authorised Version translates 'Satan hath
desired to have you . . .'; the Revised Version 'Satan asked to have
you' (margin, 'obtained you by asking' – so F. Field, in *Notes on
the Translation of the New Testament*, 'Satan has procured you');
New English Bible 'Satan has been given leave to sift all of you . . .'
If the New English Bible is right, the thought of the passage would
seem to be similar to that of *Job* 1: 12 and 2: 6, where God gives
Satan permission to go so far but no further in his testing of His
servant Job. The final issues are in the hands of God. In another
great Biblical drama, the book of the Revelation, we see demonic
powers let loose against the children of light. 'But', says H. L.
Goudge with insight, 'though it is hell let *loose*, it is hell *let* loose'
(*The Apocalypse and the Present Age*, p. 82). His point is that the
last word is with God.

ii. The *core* of the prayer is 'that thy faith fail not'. Why did
Jesus fasten on faith as the crucial point in the experience of Simon,
the point which above all others needed now to be watched? The
answer is clear. Faith is trust in another, reliance upon one other
than oneself. Peter was showing ominous signs of self-reliance. No
doubt he had taken a part, perhaps a leading part, in the un-
edifying debate as to 'who among them should rank highest' (v. 24,
N.E.B.) – had he not been among the very first to be called (*St.*

Mark 1: 16)? And there was a dangerous note of cocksureness even of bragging, about his boast, however sincere its intention, 'Lord, I am ready to go with you to prison and death' (v. 33, N.E.B.). It called forth a swift rebuke from the Master (v. 34).

Later on, the crucial point will be *love*. Crucifixion and resurrection behind, and missionary task ahead, the acid test will be the answer to the thrice repeated question, 'Simon, son of John, do you *love* Me . . .?' (*St. John* 21: 15-17, N.E.B.). Now the crucial point is *faith* – is your trust and confidence self-centred or is it orientated to the Christ of God? The prayer before the cross is as shrewd as the question after it is searching.

iii. '. . . that thy faith *fail* not.' The verb is used of years coming to an end and so of death, of money giving out, of the sun being eclipsed. Indeed *eclipse* is the root of the word used here. What had burned brightly could so easily burn low or even suffer total eclipse. The warning rings true of Christian experience. The passage of the years, the corrosion of care, the invasion of unholy ambition – any or all of these things, and a dozen others besides, tend to the eclipse of faith, of that attitude of loving trust in Another which is at the heart of Christian discipleship.

iv. The prayer to God for Simon, that his faith fail not, merges into a command to Simon – 'when you have come to yourself, you must lend strength to your brothers' (v. 32, N.E.B.). 'When you have come to yourself' – there is rebuke in that clause. 'Simon, you are beside yourself, debating where you come in the apostolic hierarchy – as if that mattered, under the very shadow of the cross! Come to yourself. Come to your senses. Turn again (R.V.); be converted (A.V.); become as a little child. Then and only then will you be of any use to your brethren.'

St. Luke 23: 34

A.V.	N.E.B.
34. Then said Jesus, Father, forgive them; for they know not what they do.	Jesus said, 'Father, forgive them; they do not know what they are doing.'

In commenting on the Lord's prayer (*St. Matthew* 6: 9 ff.), we tried to see the meaning of the clause 'forgive us our trespasses, as we forgive them that trespass against us'. We noted that this clause, alone of all the clauses in the prayer, has an explanation added in vv. 14 and 15; and that there is a parable elaborating the theme in *St. Matthew* 18: 23-35 (see p. 34.). In *Acts* 7: 60, we shall see the principle of forgiveness being worked out by St. Stephen in circumstances similar to those under which our Lord prayed (see pp. 80-81 ff.).

'Father, forgive them.' The forgiveness of sins is the most powerful therapeutic idea in the world. Hatred and resentment are the destructive factors both in society and in the souls and bodies of men. If we nurse a resentment, harbour a grudge, or fan the flames of hatred, we set up a process which warps our own souls and, very probably, will in the long run injure our bodies. If, on the other hand, we learn consistently to love and to forgive, we set in motion forces that are always constructive and health-giving. 'It is love that builds' (1 *Corinthians* 8: 1, N.E.B.).

We can only surmise what the effect of these words 'Father, forgive them', must have been on the soldiers, hardened by their calling with its dreadful tasks, accustomed to hear only oaths and curses from those whom they crucified. They must have been utterly astonished, as the words sank into their dulled consciences. But that they *effected* something in them, we need not doubt. Such words, whether uttered by our Lord on the cross, or by a servant of His like Leonard Wilson in a Japanese concentration camp, are powerful, constructive, regenerative.

'They know not what they do.' How could they, these poor ignorant soldiers, tools as they were of a cruel despotic system? How could they know that the hands and feet which they pierced were the hands and feet of the Son of God? These things were hidden from their eyes. 'The princes of this world' did not know, 'for had they known it, they would not have crucified the Lord of glory' (1 *Corinthians* 2: 8); how much less would the soldiers know! Can we blame them? Who can say? Can we blame all those who shared in the atrocities perpetrated by the Nazis before and during the last war? Fortunate it is for us that we have not got to apportion the blame, and to say whether the ignorance behind the actions was wholly culpable or not. But the point is that it was, at least in part, ignorance which led to the crucifixion – 'they *know* not'. And ignorance is darkness, for darkness is the absence of light. No wonder, then, that all down the centuries the Church has seen it as one of its main tasks to scatter darkness, to pioneer education, to open the minds of men to the light of truth. But when we look at our world today, we are tempted to feel that the Church's task is hardly begun.

St. Luke 23: 46

A.V.	N.E.B.
46. And when Jesus had cried with a loud voice, he said, Father, into thy hands I commend my spirit.	Then Jesus gave a loud cry and said, 'Father, into thy hands I commit my spirit.'

The cry of dereliction ('My God, my God, why hast Thou forsaken me?') was, as we have seen, a quotation from the Psalms (*St. Matthew* 27: 46; see p. 47). The last word from the cross, as recorded here by St. Luke, is also a quotation from the Psalms (31: 5). It would seem that it was to the hymn-book of the ancient Jewish Church that Jesus most naturally turned when He needed words in which to express His deepest feelings. For multitudes of God's people that has been true down the centuries – the Psalms have 'come alive' for them in times of national or personal agony. The Psalmists have an uncanny way of expressing the deeps of human experience and of helping those who use their words to 'hold them fast by God'.

The words of committal, spoken by the Psalmist, are, however, prefaced by our Lord with the word 'Father'. No longer is it 'My God, my God', as in the cry of dereliction. Jesus reverts to the title by which He had all His life been accustomed to address God – the title 'Father' (*St. Matthew* 6: 9; see pp. 20 ff.). The sense of Father-son relationship, so dear to Him since childhood (see *St. Luke* 2: 49), is restored. Now at last, like a little child at rest in its father's arms, He can be at peace; all is well. 'He dismissed His spirit', says St. Matthew, bringing a touch of majesty into his account (27: 50).

Is it not possible that this verse from the Psalms, prefaced by the word 'Father', had in fact been part of the evening prayer of Jesus? That, night by night, before He closed His eyes in sleep, His last conscious act was to say: 'Father, into Thy hands I commend my spirit'? Now in the final act of all, before the shadow of death falls on Him, the habit stands Him in good stead; once again, He makes the words His own – there could be none better.

This seems to be wholly likely. But whether this was the habit of Jesus or not, it is one which the disciple might well adopt. In fact, the ideal way to *begin* the day is to use this prayer, as soon as consciousness returns; before the flood of daily duties begins to make its clamour heard, before even one rises from bed, let the simple prayer go up to God: 'Father, into Thy hands I commend my spirit'. And then, the very last thing at night, just before one lapses into sleep and the mysterious forces of unconsciousness do their work, let the same prayer be said: 'Father, into Thy hands I commend my spirit'.

> 'So shall no part of day or night
> From sacredness be free;
> But all my life, in every step,
> Be fellowship with Thee.'
>
> (H. Bonar)

It is an ideal not impossible of achievement. Given this, why should we fear the advent of the last night of life — or, should we rather say, the dawn of the new day?

ST. JOHN

St. John 11: 41-42

A.V.	N.E.B.
41. And Jesus lifted up his eyes, and said, Father, I thank thee that thou hast heard me.	Then Jesus looked upwards and said, 'Father, I thank thee: thou hast heard me.
42. And I knew that thou hearest me always: but because of the people which stand by I said it, that they may believe that thou hast sent me.	I knew already that thou always hearest me, but I spoke for the sake of the people standing round, that they might believe that thou didst send me.'

THIS brief prayer cannot be understood apart from a considera-tion of the great drama of life and death in which it is set, the story of the raising of Lazarus from the dead. Two things stand out:

i. *This is a prayer uttered in the midst of grief.* The emphasis which the evangelist lays on the grief and distress of Jesus at the graveside of Lazarus is remarkable. The vehemence of that grief comes out more strongly in the original than it does in the English translation (most expecially in vv. 33-38). What was it that moved Him so deeply? No doubt it was sympathy with the sorrowing sisters – there seems to have been a very deep friendship between our Lord and the little family at Bethany. The cause of His grief may also have been the unbelief of those who stood around the cave, including Martha and Mary (vv. 21, 32). But perhaps there was more to it than this. Was it due to a feeling on the part of our Lord that death, in the case of one as young as Lazarus, was wrong – that just as He saw in the bowed form of the woman the binding of Satan (*St. Luke* 13: 16), so He saw his evil operation in the death of Lazarus? That here was something essentially wrong – to be fought and to be conquered? We are on mysterious ground here, but the forcefulness of the language used by the evangelist compels us to face the problem.

Whatever the cause, His grief is deep. What does He do? He consciously enters into communion with the Father. He withdraws – not indeed in body, but in spirit. He retreats before He advances

57

to the battle with death. Simply a lifting up of the eyes (v. 41, cp. 17: 1), and He is in touch with the Father.

ii. *This is a prayer uttered in the midst of activity*. The withdrawal is only momentary. The prayer is little more than ejaculatory. Around Him is the crowd, critical, inquisitive, grief-stricken. He has just been deeply engaged in dialogue with Martha and Mary. He is about to utter the imperatives: 'Lazarus, come forth' and 'Loose him, and let him go'. It is a scene of action. But in the midst of it is a pool of quiet – 'Father, I thank Thee . . . ' And in that quiet there comes to Him the strong assurance that the Father is there, and that He is listening. All will be well. The victory will be won. In that assurance, He faces death and brings life. 'I knew that Thou hearest me always'.

As our Lord, surrounded by obtuse disciples, uttered a prayer of thanksgiving (*St. Matthew* 11: 25-26 – *St. Luke* 10: 21; see pp. 41 ff.), so now, faced by death, He looks up and says: 'Father, I thank Thee . . .'

There is strength in the prayer of recollection, especially in the midst of grief and of intense activity.

St. John 12: 27-28

A.V.	N.E.B.
27. Now is my soul troubled; and what shall I say? Father, save me from this hour: but for this cause came I unto this hour.	'Now my soul is in turmoil, and what am I to say? Father, save me from this hour. No, it was for this that I came to this hour.
28. Father, glorify thy name.	Father, glorify thy name.'

The absence of marks of punctuation from original Greek manuscripts sometimes puts us in doubt as to the exact meaning of a passage. This is a case in point. 'Father, save me from this hour' – how do we punctuate? With a colon (as in the Authorised Version), or with a full-stop (as in the Revised Version and the New English Bible)? Or with a question mark (as in the Revised Version margin and in the New English Bible footnote)? No one can be sure. For myself, I cannot but feel that the Revised Version margin provides the most likely interpretation (for punctuation *is* here a matter of interpretation).

Jesus has reached His hour of greatest testing and turmoil – the verb in v. 27 ('is . . . troubled'; 'is in turmoil', N.E.B.) is used of a storm-tossed sea. What is He to say? All His human instincts cry out: 'Father, save me from this hour'. But will He yield to these instincts? Will He utter this prayer? 'What shall I say? Father, save me from this hour? No. Father, glorify Thy name — it was for this cause that I came to this hour.' The temptation, sharp and cruel, is resisted, thrust aside, conquered. Jesus has won. 'Thy will be done.' And the victory is ratified by a voice from heaven which says: 'I have both glorified (My name), and will glorify it again' (v. 28).

We may put it this way. The divine preposition is not 'out of' ('Father, save me *out of* this hour'), but 'through' — 'I will see you *through* this hour'. We shall find another illustration of this when we come to consider the prayer-life of St. Paul and his natural desire to be delivered *out of* the miseries brought on him by his thorn in the flesh (2 *Corinthians* 12: 1-10; see pp. 90 ff.). Christ, 'son though He was ... learned obedience in the school of suffering' (*Hebrews* 5: 8, N.E.B.). It is a lesson every disciple has to learn, too.

Into these brief sentences — 'Father, save me from this hour?' and 'Father, glorify Thy name' — are packed concepts which we consider elsewhere. References to them must suffice here:

On *Father*, see *St. Matthew* 6: 9; and pp. 19 ff.

On *hour*, see *St. John* 17; and pp. 63.

On *glorify*, see *St. John* 17; and pp. 63 ff. (and cp. 'Hallowed be Thy name', and pp. 23 ff.).

On *name*, see *St. John* 17; and pp. 69 ff.

St. John 17

A.V.	N.E.B.
1. These words spake Jesus, and lifted up his eyes to heaven, and said, Father, the hour is come; glorify thy Son, that thy Son also may glorify thee:	After these words Jesus looked up to heaven and said: 'Father, the hour has come. Glorify thy Son, that the Son may glorify thee.
2. As thou hast given him power over all flesh, that he should give eternal life to as many as thou hast given him.	For thou hast made him sovereign over all mankind, to give eternal life to all whom thou hast given him.
3. And this is life eternal, that they might know thee the only true God, and Jesus Christ, whom thou hast sent.	This is eternal life: to know thee who alone art truly God, and Jesus Christ whom thou hast sent.

A.V.

N.E.B.

4. I have glorified thee on the earth: I have finished the work which thou gavest me to do.

I have glorified thee on earth by completing the work which thou gavest me to do;

5. And now, O Father, glorify thou me with thine own self with the glory which I had with thee before the world was.

And now, Father, glorify me in thine own presence with the glory which I had with thee before the world began.

6. I have manifested thy name unto the men which thou gavest me out of the world: thine they were, and thou gavest them me; and they have kept thy word.

I have made thy name known to the men whom thou didst give me out of the world. They were thine, thou gavest them to me, and they have obeyed thy command.

7. Now they have known that all things whatsoever thou hast given me are of thee.

Now they know that all thy gifts have come to me from thee;

8. For I have given unto them the words which thou gavest me; and they have received them, and have known surely that I came out from thee, and they have believed that thou didst send me.

For I have taught them all that I learned from thee, and they have received it: they know with certainty that I came from thee; they have had faith to believe that thou didst send me.

9. I pray for them: I pray not for the world, but for them which thou hast given me; for they are thine.

I pray for them; I am not praying for the world but for those whom thou hast given me, because they belong to thee.

10. And all mine are thine, and thine are mine; and I am glorified in them.

All that is mine is thine, and what is thine is mine; and through them has my glory shone.

11. And now I am no more in the world, but these are in the world, and I come to thee. Holy Father, keep through thine own name those whom thou hast given me, that they may be one, as we are.

I am to stay no longer in the world, but they are still in the world, and I am on my way to thee. Holy Father, protect by the power of thy name those whom thou hast given me, that they may be one, as we are one.

12. While I was with them in the world, I kept them in thy name: those that thou gavest me I have kept, and none of them is lost, but the son of perdition; that the scripture might be fulfilled.

When I was with them, I protected by the power of thy name those whom thou hast given me, and kept them safe. Not one of them is lost except the man who must be lost, for Scripture has to be fulfilled.

A.V.

N.E.B.

13. And now come I to thee; and these things I speak in the world, that they might have my joy fulfilled in themselves.

And now I am coming to thee; but while I am still in the world I speak these words, so that they may have my joy within them in full measure.

14. I have given them thy word; and the world hath hated them, because they are not of the world, even as I am not of the world.

I have delivered thy word to them, and the world hates them because they are strangers in the world, as I am.

15. I pray not that thou shouldest take them out of the world, but that thou shouldest keep them from the evil.

I pray thee, not to take them out of the world, but to keep them from the evil one.

16. They are not of the world, even as I am not of the world.

They are strangers in the world, as I am.

17. Sanctify them through thy truth: thy word is truth.

Consecrate them by the truth; thy word is truth.

18. As thou hast sent me into the world, even so have I also sent them into the world.

As thou hast sent me into the world, I have sent them into the world,

19. And for their sakes I sanctify myself, that they also might be sanctified through the truth.

And for their sake I now consecrate myself, that they too may be consecrated by the truth.

20. Neither pray I for these alone, but for them also which shall believe on me through their word;

But it is not for these alone that I pray, but for those also who through their words put their faith in me;

21. That they all may be one; as thou, Father, art in me, and I in thee, that they also may be one in us: that the world may believe that thou hast sent me.

May they all be one: as thou, Father, art in me, and I in thee, so also may they be in us, that the world may believe that thou didst send me.

22. And the glory which thou gavest me I have given them; that they may be one, even as we are one:

The glory which thou gavest me I have given to them, that they may be one, as we are one;

23. I in them, and thou in me, that they may be made perfect in one; and that the world may know that thou hast sent me, and hast loved them, as thou hast loved me.

I in them and thou in me, may they be perfectly one. Then the world will learn that thou didst send me, that thou didst love them as thou didst me.

A.V.	N.E.B.
24. Father, I will that they also, whom thou hast given me, be with me where I am; that they may behold my glory, which thou hast given me: for thou lovedst me before the foundation of the world.	Father, I desire that these men, who are thy gift to me, may be with me where I am, so that they may look upon my glory, which thou hast given me because thou didst love me before the world began.
25. O righteous Father, the world hath not known thee: but I have known thee, and these have known that thou hast sent me.	O righteous Father, although the world does not know thee, I know thee, and these men know that thou didst send me.
26. And I have declared unto them thy name, and will declare it: that the love wherewith thou hast loved me may be in them, and I in them.	I made thy name known to them, and will make it known, so that the love thou hadst for me may be in them, and I may be in them.'

The fourth Evangelist places this, the longest and most penetrating of all the New Testament prayers, immediately after the three great chapters of discourse in which Jesus strengthens the disciples with the promise of the gift of the Holy Spirit after His own physical withdrawal. Having concentrated His attention on them and their needs, He turns His eyes to heaven and addresses the Father, before He marches out to death and resurrection.

The prayer is marked by extraordinary simplicity of language. But that is a mark of the whole of the Fourth Gospel. This, the profoundest of the Gospels, uses elementary language because it deals with the elemental things – life and light and bread and water and words, and so on. There is about the Gospel – and even more so about the First Epistle – a repetitiousness which could become monotonous if we did not realise that these are writings not to be read through in a hurry, but to be pondered and meditated on at leisure. What is true of Gospel and Epistles is certainly true of the chapter we are now to consider. It must be taken slowly, sentence by sentence, almost word by word, if it is to yield its inner meaning. Above all, it must be prayed as well as studied.

Probably the most helpful way in which to approach this prayer will not be to provide a verse by verse commentary, but rather to concentrate our attention on certain recurring themes, such as *hour*, *glory* (and *glorify*), *the men whom Thou hast given me*, *the world, the Name, sanctify, one*. As these themes are pondered, the meaning of the prayer will begin to unfold itself.

But first we must notice that there is a certain *shape* to the prayer. The concern of Jesus, as it is expressed to the Father (vv. 1, 5, 24), to the holy Father (v. 11), to the righteous Father (v. 25), may be thought of in terms of three circles, each wider than the others in its outreach. The *first* circle is concerned with Jesus Himself, and occupies vv. 1-5. The *second* circle is concerned with the immediate followers of Jesus, the friends around Him; this occupies vv. 6-19. The *third* circle is concerned with the Church that is to be, and occupies vv. 20-26. The divisions are not entirely 'watertight', but they serve to indicate the expanding outreach of the prayer and concern of Jesus.

We turn, then, to some of the major themes of the prayer.

i. The *hour* (v. 1). The fourth Gospel is heavy with this theme from first to last. When, at the Cana wedding-feast, the Mother of Jesus pointed out to Him that there was no wine left, Jesus mysteriously replied that His 'hour' had not yet arrived (2: 4). When the people of Jerusalem tried to seize Jesus after He had taught in the Temple, they found themselves unable to do so, because His 'hour' had not yet come (7: 30; 8: 20). 'Not yet, not yet' is the repeated note of the first half of the Gospel. But when we reach the story of 12: 20 ff. we find a change – 'the hour has come' (12: 23, 27). It is the story of the coming of some Greeks to Jesus, introduced to Him by Philip and Andrew – 'Sir, we should like to see Jesus'. It was symbolic of the fact that the work of Jesus was to be effective not only for the Jews but for the Gentiles also. The solitary grain of His life, falling into the ground and dying, would bear a rich harvest. 'I, if I be lifted up from the earth, will draw all men unto Me' (v. 32). The passion is predominant from this point on – the 'hour' had come. So it is at the beginning of chapter 13 – the *Passover* festival, the festival of sacrifice, was upon them, and 'Jesus knew that His hour had come and He must leave this world . . .' So it is at the beginning of the prayer of chapter 17 – His death is imminent, but before He goes to it He will lift His eyes to the Father in loving intercession.

ii. *Glory* and *glorify*. We are introduced to the idea of 'glory' towards the end of the prologue of St. John. That prologue opens with the tremendous theme of the Word of God, through whom creation took its being, in whom were light and life. The theme, outlined with a kind of monosyllabic majesty, works up to the climactic verse 14: 'the Word was made flesh, and tabernacled among us' (lived His life in the body as in a tent), 'and we beheld His . . .' – how would you have completed that sentence if you had been the writer? 'We beheld His humiliation', surely; for, as St. Paul put it, He 'made Himself of no reputation, and took upon Him the form of a servant . . . He humbled Himself, and became obedient unto death, even the death of the cross' (*Philippians* 2: 7-8). 'We beheld His humiliation'. Not so St. John. He writes: 'We beheld His *glory*, the glory as of the only begotten of the Father . . .'

Here is paradox, if ever there was paradox. 'Flesh – glory'; this is the divine economy. And here is the clue to the understanding of much that is fundamental in the writing of St. John. He would say to us that, if we want to understand the meaning of glory, we shall find it, not surrounded by the traditional paraphernalia of angels and clouds of brilliance and voices of thunder, but rather in a manger, at a carpenter's bench, and on a cross.

One of the most formative concepts of the Old Testament was the idea that God deigned to dwell with His people in the tabernacle. It was the centre of the manifestation of the glory of God to all the people. The book of Exodus (40: 34 ff.) records that, after the tabernacle had been reared, 'a cloud covered the tent of the congregation, and the glory of the Lord filled the tabernacle'. Especially at the hour of sacrifice was this presence manifested (*Leviticus* 9: 6, 23). So it was at the Incarnation, when the Word, made flesh, 'tabernacled among us'. At the moment of divine humiliation and sacrifice, the glory was seen, but veiled with the cloud of human flesh.

When, just above, we considered the concept of 'the hour', we noted how, in chapter 12, the coming of the Greeks to Jesus was a turning point in His ministry. 'The hour is come, that the Son of Man should be *glorified*' (v. 23). If we ask what Jesus means by that verb, we are not left in doubt, for immediately He speaks of the corn of wheat falling into the ground and dying; of hating one's life and so keeping it for life eternal. And when, in vv. 27 and 28, we are given the Johannine parallel to the Synoptic story of the agony in Gethsemane, and Jesus battles His way through till He can pray 'Father, glorify Thy name', the reply comes back, 'I have both glorified it, and will glorify it again' – the sacrifice is accepted, and the story sweeps on to the cross.

With chapter 13 comes the story of the foot-washing, the supreme example of the humility of service. Then, the departure of Judas; 'and it was night' (v. 30). Abysmal treachery on the part

of one of the inner circle of the men He had loved and trained;
desperate lack of understanding on the part of the other eleven —
'Lord, where are you going?' . . . 'Lord, why cannot I follow you
now?' 'Before the cock crows you will have denied Me three times'
(vv. 36-38, N.E.B.). And in the midst of *that* — glory! Five times
over in the space of two verses comes the verb — 'Now the Son of
Man is glorified, and in Him God is glorified. If God is glorified in
Him, God will also glorify Him in Himself; and He will glorify
Him now' (vv. 31, 32, N.E.B.). The darker the shadow cast by the
cross, the brighter the light of the glory becomes.

When we come to the High Priestly prayer of chapter 17, we see
Jesus on the very threshold of His final act of humiliation; the
offering for us men and for our salvation is just about to be made.
He has become 'obedient unto death, even the death of the cross'.
But glory shines through the prayer with a radiance all the brighter
for the nearness of the offering. 'Father, the hour is come; glorify
Thy Son, that Thy Son also may glorify Thee' (v. 1). Dr. Vincent
Taylor has put it well: 'For the Fourth Gospel . . . the humiliation
of the cross has practically disappeared; it is no longer a *skandalon*
(stumbling-block) but a shining stairway by which the Son of God
ascends to His Father'.

It is clear that this paradox is central to the whole Gospel, and it
accounts for the vehemence of certain passages in the discourses
of Jesus where the subject of glory, true and false, is under discussion. In chapter 5, the Jews are accused (v. 44), in contrast to
our Lord (v. 41), of receiving glory from one another, and of
failing to seek the glory that comes from the only God (cf. the
charge against the Pharisees in 12: 43). A similar charge (and
contrast) is made in 7: 18 and in 8: 50, 54. The reason for the
vehemence of Jesus is not far to seek. The Jews showed a complete
lack of appreciation of the basic principle of the Incarnation, of the
whole 'scheme of things' as seen through the eyes of God, that if
we want to know the meaning of glory we shall find it in the
service which is characterised by humiliation to the uttermost.

Jesus gave to His men the glory which God had given Him
(v. 22) — the glory of unity such as belonged to the Father and the
Son, unity of will and of purpose, manifesting itself in costly self-
giving for the salvation of the world. That is the only glory He
knew. It was the only glory for them.[1]

iii. *The men whom Thou hast given me* (vv. 6, 9, 11, 24; cf. v. 2).

[1] In this section on *glory* and *glorify*, I have drawn on my little book *The
Glory of God* (C.M.S., 1950).

They were all He had – a gift of incomparable worth from the Father to the Son. What could He do for them? He could not endow them, for He had no money. He could not entertain them, for He had no place to lay His head. Two things He could do for them – He could *train* them, and He could *pray* for them. We look at these separately:

(a) *Training*. It is clear from a reading of the Gospels that the training of the Twelve occupied a large part of the ministry of Jesus. The content of that training is suggested in this prayer. He gave them what may be called *experiential religion* – 'I have taught them all that I learned from Thee' (v. 8, N.E.B.). This was no cold theorising. This was the religion of Jesus Himself, His knowledge of the Father, His love of the Father, His insights into the meaning of the reign of God, shared with His men. Further, He gave them the doctrine of His own Person – 'that I came from Thee' – and they 'had faith to believe . . .' (v. 8, N.E.B.). Thus the faith was taught and caught; what was a vivid reality to Him became a vivid reality to them. Again, He gave them 'Thy word' (v. 14); the sacred principles of truth committed to Him He handed on to them. This is training of the first order – truth illuminated, made alive, by experience.

(b) *Prayer*. If we ask *what* He prayed for them, three things stand out in this chapter. *First*, He prayed for protection for them – 'protect by the power of Thy name those whom Thou hast given me'; 'I pray Thee . . . to keep them from the evil one' (vv. 11, 15, N.E.B.). He knew that anyone who espouses His cause becomes at once a target for special attack. Temptations of pride; temptations to split up into warring parties (note 'protect . . . that they may be one', v. 11, N.E.B.); these and a hundred other temptations, subtle as well as crude, would attack body, mind and spirit. Hence the prayer for protection. *Secondly* – and this may be a matter of surprise to some – He prayed for joy for them (v. 13). The request is peculiarly phrased – 'the joy which is My own'. He is not asking for the world's joy for them, a kind of joy which is dependent on success or popularity or any such thing; but for *My* joy, that is to say, the joy of doing the will of God and of being utterly satisfied with Him. *Thirdly*, He prays that these men 'may be with me where I am' (v. 24). This is not simply a prayer that He and they may be together in heaven, to be separated no more. This is also a prayer for the present. It is a prayer which, if expressed in terms of chapter 15, would be that there should be no separation between Vine and branches, but that, in the arid atmosphere of 'the world', the life-giving sap of the Vine might so flow into the branches that much fruit would be borne. The disciple need not wait for heaven to 'look upon' the glory of Jesus (v. 24). *Protection*, *joy*, and *close union*—this is the burden of the prayer of Jesus for the men God had given Him.

The phrase 'the men whom Thou hast given me' has, in this context, a unique significance. The One to whom these men were given was the Saviour of the world, very God of very God, the only begotten of the Father. And 'the men' were the apostolic band, the nucleus of the new Israel, the men who had continued with the Master in His temptations and to whom He appointed a kingdom (*St. Luke* 22: 28-30).

But in the mystery and grace of God's dealing with His people, there are secondary senses in which *we* may use the phrase – 'the men whom Thou didst give *me* . . .'

When a bishop ordains a man, he, under God, initiates a relationship which is of this order. The men ordained are men whom God has given him out of the world. So it is, though in not quite such an intimacy as exists between the bishop and those whom he has personally ordained, with the bishop and all his clergy. They are the men whom God has given him out of the world – to pray for, to care for, to teach, to shepherd, to guide, to govern. And as he goes to a Quiet Day or Retreat for the Women Workers or the Readers of the diocese, he realises that they are the women, the men, whom God has given him out of the world.

Nor is this relationship confined to the episcopal office, though it is found there in a very special intimacy and sacredness. Here is an incumbent training a class of confirmees. Their Christian background may be very shaky, their comprehension of the Christian faith very limited. But they are the people whom in a special sense God has given him, and they constitute a very sacred trust.

Or here is a preacher. His congregation is small and, he is tempted to think, not very bright. Is it worth the candle week by week to prepare carefully a message which in some way will declare to them the mind and will of God? Why not by-pass the preaching? But he cannot, for these are the men and women whom God has given him. He is responsible to God for them. They are a sacred trust.

Or here is a parent. The training of young people in the ways of the Christian faith seems to him to be fraught with difficulties which become greater as the years pass. The forces of secularism press in ever more mercilessly. 'Say not the struggle nought availeth' — yes, he knows Clough's lines, but he is sorely tempted to disobey them! Then he remembers. These children of his are the men (in the making) whom God has given him. He cannot fail a God who has thus trusted him.

iv. *The world.* The men whom the Father gave to Jesus are described as given to Him 'out of the world'. What does St. John mean by 'the world'? Bishop Gore used to describe it as 'society organised apart from God', and that is a good enough definition for what in the Johannine writings is a major concept. It is the transitory as compared with what abides — 'the world passeth away, and the lust thereof: but he that doeth the will of God abideth for ever' (1 *St. John* 2: 17). It is the order, with all its glitter and show, which the natural man thinks most important. It is 'the worldling's pleasure, all its boasted pomp and show' which contrasts with the 'solid joys and lasting treasures' which 'none but Zion's children know'. The evil one is described as 'the prince of this world' who found nothing in Jesus on which he could fasten to despoil Him (*St. John* 14: 30). And yet the same word (*kosmos*) is used by St. John when he tells us that God *loved* the world (*St. John* 3: 16). True, it by-passed Him. True, it got its values and priorities wrong. But God loved it enough to give His Son to die for it.

Now, the men whom God has given to Jesus are still 'in the world' (v. 11). They have their responsibilities to Caesar as well as to God (*St. Mark* 12: 17). They must not seek to contract out of such responsibilities into an other-worldly and false isolationism. But at the same time they are 'out of the world' — the preposition indicates *separateness from* the world. While they are *in* it, they are not wholly *of* it. That is to say, there is a dividing line between Church and world, and woe betide the Church and its witness if that line becomes blurred. Here precisely is the tension in which the Church finds itself, in which every Christian finds himself, inexorably involved; and the success — we had better put it, the health — of his Christian life and witness depends on the measure in which he maintains that tension. He is a follower of the incarnate Lord, who plunged into the midst of this world and its affairs, who went to the Cana wedding-party, who mixed with all strata of society and especially with the tax-gathers and disreputables, and at the last died between two ruffians. He was '*in* the world', totally involved with sinners. But He was also 'separate from sinners'

(*Hebrews* 7: 26), undefiled by His contacts with the likes of us, untouched by any breath of scandal, utterly pure.

This is the tension of the Christian life — to be 'in the world', indeed to rejoice in being there; but at the same time always to remember that as the men whom God has given to Christ we are called 'out of the world'.

v. *The Name* (vv. 6, 11, 12, 26). The name to a Hebrew meant much more than it does to a Westerner. The Old Testament is full of illustrations of that. To know the name of a person was to be in touch with his person and the secret of his power. Thus it is crucial to Moses to know the Name of God if he is to be His messenger to the children of Israel, and the disclosure to Moses of the Name of Yahweh ('I will be what I will be') was an event of supreme importance in the revelation of the Old Testament (*Exodus* 3: 11 ff.). (See, further, on *St. Matthew* 6: 9 and note pp. 23 ff.) So, when in vv. 11 and 12, the New English Bible substitutes 'by the power of Thy name' for the Authorised and Revised versions 'through Thine own name' and 'in Thy name', it only expresses what is inherent in the phrase.

Twice in this prayer Jesus declares that He has made God's name known to the men whom God has given to Him (vv. 6, 26; cf. v. 14). He has shown them what God is like. In seeing Him, they have seen the Father (*St. John* 14: 9). His own character and His verbal teaching about God have been in perfect harmony in the revelation of the nature of God. But the work was not complete; it had to be continued — 'I will make it known' (v. 26). How will this be? 'Upon the cross', says Archbishop William Temple, tersely (*Readings in St. John's Gospel*, p. 331). That is true, for there was the supreme manifestation of the heart and mind of God. But it is not only there. Must we not add: 'through the Church'? For it is the first task of the Church to 'manifest the name' of God, to make His character known in its holiness and its majesty.

It should, therefore, be the ambition of the Christian disciple to be able to say, in some measure at least, at the end of every day: 'I have manifested Thy name'. In so far as he is not able to say this, there is cause for repentance and for the seeking of forgiveness. So, when he stands to speak on his Master's behalf, it should be his ambition to be able to say at the end of the address: 'I have manifested the name of God, I have made clear some aspect of His character to those who have listened'. Or again, when some chapter of experience in life is drawing to a close (a clerical incumbency or a secular post), it should be our ambition to be able in some way to echo the words of Jesus: 'I have manifested Thy name'. The success or failure of our life at its end will be measured by the degree in which it is possible to utter these words.

vi. *Sanctify* (*consecrate*, N.E.B.). The verb occurs twice in this prayer – at vv. 17 and 19.

Under the third of these themes ('the men whom Thou hast given me'), we noted that the two main things that our Lord did for His men was to train them and to pray for them. If we ask why He thus concentrated His care on them, we find that it was that they might be 'sanctified' or 'consecrated'. The verb 'to consecrate' has in the Old Testament a strong sacrificial flavour. It is used of setting things aside and making them suitable for ritual purposes, and of dedicating persons to special work (as, e.g. in *Exodus* 28: 41). So it is here. Jesus looked toward the sacrifice of the Cross – it was for them, 'that they may be consecrated'.

As with the Master, so it should be with the disciple. Whenever we share in that meal in which the passion of Jesus is, as it were, re-enacted, we do it not merely for our own sakes, for our own comfort or strengthening, but 'for their sakes' (v. 19). Participation in the Holy Communion is not a luxury for the devout. It is preparation for sacrifice and for battle. The eyes of the worshipper are not centred on himself, but on his Lord and on those for whom He died, that 'they may be sanctified by the truth'. In those moments which follow the reception of the elements and which for some have about them a sense of bathos, we may make the prayer of Jesus our own, thus filling the time with profitable dedication and intercession. 'For their sakes', we pray, 'we consecrate ourselves – for the sake of our family, our dearest and our best; for the parish to which we belong; for those to whom this day we shall minister in word or sacrament or Sunday School or Bible class; for the Rural Deanery of which our parish is a part; for the diocese and Bishop; for the Province; for the Anglican Communion; for the whole Church of God of which the Anglican Communion is a part; for the world for which Christ died.' So in ever-widening circles, the prayer of consecration goes out – 'for their sakes'.

vii. *One*. Our Lord's prayer for unity occurs four times in this chapter – once in the section in which he is concerned with the circle of friends then around Him (v. 11), and thrice in the section where He prays for the Church that is to be (vv. 21, 22, 23). About this unity we may ask two questions, and find the answers at least adumbrated here.

(a) *What kind of unity was in the mind of Jesus?* He prays 'that they may be one, *as we are one*' (v. 11, cp. vv. 21, 23). The mutual love of Father and Son was the basis of their unity. The never-ebbing passion to know and do the will of the Father was the basis of His unity with Him. This is the unity for which He prays for the men whom God had given Him and was to give Him—a unity of love and desire.

(b) *What was the purpose of this unity for which He prayed?* The answer is twofold. The *first* purpose is evangelistic — 'that the world may believe that Thou hast sent me' (v. 21); 'that the world may know . . .' (v. 23; 'learn', N.E.B.). A disunited Church is a Church evangelistically enfeebled. A divided world will give little heed to the voice of a divided Church. The *second* purpose is that they (the men 'whom Thou hast given me') 'may be with me where I am; that they may behold my glory' (v. 24). On the phrase 'be with me where I am', see pp. 66-67. And on 'glory', see pp. 63 ff. To 'behold' means, in St. John, to 'share in' (cp. 3: 36, though the verb used there — to 'see life' — is different from the one used here). This, then, is a prayer for shared glory, which, as we have seen, means also shared suffering. The prayer is thus close to the ambition expressed by St. Paul in *Philippians* 3: 10, 'that I may know Him, and the power of His resurrection, and the fellowship of His sufferings . . .' (cp. *Romans* 8: 17).

This great High-Priestly Prayer of *St. John* 17 is for use by the Church. One of the most fruitful ways of using it is to do so, verse by verse, in close conjunction with the Lord's Prayer. How this may be done has been shown by the Rev. John Neale in *Litany of Jesus Praying*, which is printed, by the author's kind permission, as an appendix to this book (pp. 186 ff.).

St. John 19: 28

A.V.	N.E.B.
28. After this, Jesus knowing that all things were now accomplished, that the scripture might be fulfilled, saith, I thirst.	After that, Jesus, aware that all had now come to its appointed end, said in fulfilment of Scripture, 'I thirst.'

The fourth evangelist gives us two of the seven words from the cross — 'I thirst' and 'It is finished'. It would be quite possible to maintain that in no sense is either of these words addressed to God and that therefore they should no more find a place in this book than the words 'Woman, behold thy son' and 'Today thou shalt be with me in paradise'. In the case of the word 'I thirst', it could be argued, this is simply a statement of dreadful fact. There is nothing more to it than that.

Such an argument should not be lightly dismissed. We ought not to shut our eyes to the appalling agony of crucifixion, with its attendant torture of parched throat and tongue. 'I thirst' was undoubtedly a cry of physical agony, and the soldiers acted rightly, in their own crude way, in soaking a sponge in wine, fixing it on a javelin, and holding it up to our Lord's lips (*St. John* 19: 29, N.E.B.). Nor did Jesus disdain to accept this kindly act – He received the wine, before uttering the word 'It is finished'.

But I am not convinced that this is all there is to it – that it was simply a cry directed from the Man on the cross to the men standing around its foot. As I listen to that cry, I think I can hear another note in it – not this time a note of physical torture addressed to men, but a note of spiritual aspiration addressed to God. All His life Jesus had been consumed by a passion – call it a thirst, if you will – to do the will of God. The Gospels are eloquent with the theme. 'I must be about my Father's business' (*St. Luke* 2: 49); 'I must work the works of Him that sent Me, while it is day: the night cometh, when no man can work' (*St. John* 9: 4); 'My meat is to do the will of Him that sent Me, and to finish His work' (*St. John* 4: 34), and so on. Now, right at the end, this passion does not leave Him, nor will it do so until He has been enabled to cry, as He will do very shortly, 'it is finished'.

The word 'I thirst' has frequently been interpreted as our Lord's cry of yearning for the souls of men – a slightly narrower concept than the one just expounded. This may well be a true interpretation, if 'souls' be understood in no pietistic sense but as meaning the eternal welfare of men as human beings. 'I am come that they might have life, and that they might have it more abundantly' – so St. John (10: 10) expounds the purpose of the advent of Jesus. It was to put men and women in the way of this abundant life that He had preached and taught and healed and prayed. For this He had consecrated Himself, and now for this He finally offers Himself. 'I thirst' – for them.

Is there more to it than this? No doubt there is, if we had but the eyes to see. Is this a cry of self-identification of the perfect Man with sinful men in their yearnings all down the ages? Man is so made that, at his best, he thirsts – thirsts for love, thirsts for wisdom, thirsts for knowledge, thirsts for mastery over elements which so far have proved unconquerable. He is never wholly satisfied. His tragedy is that he seeks to slake his thirst, all too often, at waters that prove brackish and bitter. But we may well believe that the thirst itself is one divinely implanted, and, moreover, one that can only be satisfied in God Himself. The whole ministry — the whole incarnate life of Jesus — was one of identification with human kind. 'He shared our flesh and blood', says the writer of the Epistle to the Hebrews (see 2: 14, N.E.B.). Must He not have shared our thirst, too? And shared it right to the end?

St. John 19: 30

A.V.	N.E.B.
30. When Jesus therefore had received the vinegar, he said, It is finished: and he bowed his head, and gave up the ghost.	Having received the wine, he said, 'It is accomplished!' He bowed his head and gave up his spirit.

Again, as in the case of the word 'I thirst', this word 'It is finished' could be simply the statement of a brutal fact. It could — if the translation 'it is finished' is, in fact, an adequate rendering of the original. 'It is all over' could practically mean '*I* am finished', as a man might say who was beaten in battle, a man for whom the opposing forces had proved too strong. 'I am done for — finished!' In that case, this muttered cry is an admission of defeat — muttered to the men who had murdered Him. This is the end — they can take the Body down and bury it.

But the arguments against such an interpretation are overwhelmingly strong. St. Matthew (27: 50), though he does not record the *words* of the last cry from the cross, says that it was a loud one. So does St. Mark (15: 37). And so does St. Luke (23: 46), though he intimates that after the cry came the prayer of committal and then the end. If St. John provides the words of the cry to which St. Matthew and St. Mark refer, this was no last gasp of defeat. It was something much more like a cry of victory.

But there is a stronger argument. Jesus presumably said this word in Aramaic. But St. John translates it in such a way that it can only mean what the New English Bible gives as its meaning — 'It is *accomplished*!' This is the end — yes; but not in terms of terminus but of achievement. This is what the runner says when he has breasted the tape before all his fellow-competitors — 'accomplished'. This is what the artist says when, having laboured at his creative work over long weeks and months, he has nothing more to add, but can stand back and say 'Accomplished! Finished!' This is an echo of the prayer in *St. John* 17: 4, 'I have glorified thee on earth *by completing the work* which thou gavest me to do' (N.E.B.), a prayer which itself is echoed in the prayer of consecration in the Holy Communion service—He 'made there (by His one oblation of Himself once offered) a full, perfect, and sufficient sacrifice, oblation, and satisfaction, for the sins of the whole world . . .'

> 'Love's redeeming work is done;
> Fought the fight, the battle won:
> Lo, our Sun's eclipse is o'er!
> Lo, He sets in blood no more!'
>
> (Charles Wesley)

John Masefield, near the end of his play, 'The Trial of Jesus', has a fine passage in which he in imagination records a conversation between Procula, the wife of Pilate, and Longinus, the centurion who stood by the cross.

> Longinus says: 'He wasn't a strong man. The scourging must have nearly killed him. I thought he was dead by morning and then suddenly he began to sing in a loud clear voice that he was giving back his spirit to God. I looked to see God come to take him. He died singing. Truly, lady, that man was the Son of God, if one may say that'.

A little later, the play goes on:

> Longinus: 'He was a fine young fellow, my lady, not past the middle age. And he was all alone and defied all the Jews and all the Romans, and when we had done with him, he was a poor broken-down thing, dead on the cross.'
> Procula: 'Do you think he is dead?'
> Longinus: 'No, lady, I don't.'
> Procula: 'Then where is he?'
> Longinus: 'Let loose in the world, lady, where neither Roman nor Jew can stop his truth.'

That is not a bad interpretation of this great triumphant cry from the cross.

THE PRAYERS IN THE ACTS OF
THE APOSTLES

THERE are no great prayers recorded in *The Acts of the Apostles*, if 'great' is to be understood in the sense that we should call the Lord's Prayer (*St. Matthew* 6: 9 ff.) or the High Priestly Prayer (*St. John* 17) or the prayers of St. Paul's Epistles great. But the study of the half-dozen or so which are scattered in this book is not to be neglected or by-passed for that reason. In studying these prayers we overhear the Church at work – the Church in the sense of an ordinary cross-section of Christian disciples faced with a variety of situations and problems which drove them to their knees.

It does not take a great deal of imagination to see the modern counterparts of the situations reflected in these prayers. The early Christians engaging in the choice of one to fill an important office (1: 24-25); a persecuted minority at prayer (4: 24-30 – should not this prayer help us in self-identification with our brethren in countries where there is active or 'cold' opposition to Christianity?); a martyr facing death (7: 59-60); a man at the crisis point of his conversion (9: 5); a good man terrified at the prospect of a duty facing him (9: 10, 13-14); an apostle refusing to face the cost of new truth (10: 14) – this may be ancient Church history; but it is much more. It is the Church, in all its frailty, in all its perplexity, going to its Lord in prayer. It is the Church doing what it is made to do – having intercourse with its Lord.

As we study these prayers, we pray: 'Lord, teach us to pray as You taught them'.

Acts 1: 24-25

A.V.	N.E.B.
24. Thou, Lord, which knowest the hearts of all men, shew whether of these two thou hast chosen,	'Thou, Lord, who knowest the hearts of all men, declare which of these two thou hast chosen
25. That he may take part of this ministry and apostleship, from which Judas by transgression fell, that he might go to his own place.	To receive this office of ministry and apostleship which Judas abandoned to go where he belonged.'

It seems strange to us that, in so big a decision as the choosing of a successor to Judas in the apostolic band, the method of lots should have been used (v. 26). We may note that this is the last recorded decision of the followers of Jesus before Pentecost, and that the method of casting lots is never recorded in the New Testament as having been used after Pentecost. It may well be that such a means of finding divine guidance was clearly seen to have been superseded when the Holy Spirit had been given. Anyhow, it was but an adjunct to prayer. Prayer preceded it.

Both Joseph (also known as Barsabbas and who bore the added name of Justus) and Matthias are described in vv. 21 and 22 as men who bore company with the apostolic band all the while the Lord Jesus was with them, from John's ministry of baptism until the day of the Ascension. Yet neither of them is so much as mentioned by name in any of the four Gospels! This is a wholesome reminder to us of how very partial a record the Gospels give of much that we most want to know in the story of the incarnate life of our Lord. The Gospels are not biographies in any sense of the modern use of that term. They are fragmentary records made largely for purposes of preaching and teaching and, probably especially, for use at gatherings for public worship.

These two men, Joseph Barsabbas and Matthias, both met the requirement of having companied with Jesus. Which of them was the right one for this particular office and work? The 'assembled brotherhood, about one hundred and twenty in all' (v. 15, N.E.B.) betook themselves to prayer at the instigation of St. Peter, prayer made all the more solemn by the remembrance of Judas' tragic end. The prayer was admirably simple. God knows men's hearts, as men can never do. May that God, 'to whom all hearts be open, all desires known', make His will manifest. That was all. It was enough.

The idea of God's looking on the heart, whereas men often could do little better than look on the outward appearance, was a familiar one to the 'brotherhood', from many an Old Testament story and reference. One thinks, for example, of Eliab's appearance before Samuel, and of Samuel's certainty that this was the Lord's anointed. 'But the Lord said unto Samuel, Look not on his countenance, or on the height of his stature; because I have refused him: for the Lord seeth not as man seeth; for man looketh on the outward appearance, but the Lord looketh on the heart' (1 *Samuel* 16: 7). Again one thinks of Jeremiah's searching words: 'I the Lord search the heart, I try the reins, even to give every man according to his ways, and according to the fruit of his doings' (*Jeremiah* 17: 10).

But, better even than this, the early Christians had the example of their Lord who, before the choice of the Twelve, 'went out into a mountain to pray, and continued all night in prayer to God' (*St. Luke* 6: 12 ff.; see pp. 16-17). It would seem that the brotherhood had learnt their lesson from Him.

Acts 4: 24-30

A.V.	N.E.B.
24. Lord, thou art God, which hast made heaven, and earth, and the sea, and all that in them is:	'Sovereign Lord, maker of heaven and earth and sea and of everything in them,
25. Who by the mouth of thy servant David hast said, Why did the heathen rage, and the people imagine vain things?	Who by the Holy Spirit, through the mouth of David thy servant, didst say, "Why did the Gentiles rage and the peoples lay their plots in vain?
26. The kings of the earth stood up, and the rulers were gathered together against the Lord, and against his Christ.	The kings of the earth took their stand and the rulers made common cause Against the Lord and against his Messiah."
27. For of a truth against thy holy child Jesus, whom thou hast anointed, both Herod, and Pontius Pilate, with the Gentiles, and the people of Israel, were gathered together,	They did indeed make common cause in this very city against thy holy servant Jesus whom thou didst anoint as Messiah. Herod and Pontius Pilate conspired with the Gentiles and peoples of Israel
28. For to do whatsoever thy hand and thy counsel determined before to be done.	To do all the things which, under thy hand and by thy decree, were foreordained.
29. And now, Lord, behold their threatenings: and grant unto thy servants, that with all boldness they may speak thy word,	And now, O Lord, mark their threats, and enable thy servants to speak thy word with all boldness.
30. By stretching forth thine hand to heal; and that signs and wonders may be done by the name of thy holy child Jesus.	Stretch out thy hand to heal and cause signs and wonders to be done through the name of thy holy servant Jesus.'

The background of this prayer is the story of the healing of the lame man (3: 1 ff.), of Peter's sermon (3: 12-26), of the imprisonment of Peter and John and of the court case that followed (4: 1-12). The people were amazed at the healing which had taken place and at the preaching of untrained laymen. On being charged to speak and teach no more in the name of Jesus, Peter replied boldly that obedience to such a command was impossible — 'we cannot but speak the things which we have seen and heard' (4: 20). There was little that the authorities could do but discharge them; and so they reported back to the brethren, who betook themselves to united prayer. To this prayer we now turn.

God is addressed as 'Sovereign Lord, maker of heaven and earth and sea and of everything in them'. It is a fuller version of the phrase used by our Lord in *St. Matthew* 11: 25, 'Father, Lord of heaven and earth' (see p. 41). God is the God of nature, powerful in His majesty. But He is also the God of revelation, as the reference in the following verses indicates — He 'spake by the prophets', He spake through the Psalmist (vv. 25 ff.). The quotation is from Psalm 2, vv. 1-2. God's 'anointed' is here identified with the Jesus Whom those addressed had so recently known in the flesh. He is twice referred to as the 'holy servant' of God (vv. 27, 30). The word here used (*pais*) can mean both *son* (A.V. has 'child') and *servant*. (Those who know their Africa will recall how the word 'boy' can be used of the son of the household and of the servant of the household.) The word is an apt one to use of our Lord who was both Son of God and, in a fuller sense than even Isaiah had dreamed, Servant of God.

To say that the events which led up to and included Good Friday were simply the result of the machinations of a petty king and a Roman governor, of Gentiles and Jews (v. 27), would be such an over-simplification of history as to be a distortion and a falsification. Looking back on those fearful events, the early Christians were constrained to say that *God* had a part in them. It was, in a real though mysterious fashion, 'under His hand and by His decree' that it happened. He took the blackest event of history and fashioned out of it His great design and worked His sovereign will. The dreadful tragedy of man's sin became the vehicle of God's victory.

The heart of the prayer is found in verses 29-30. Perhaps the request that God will 'mark the threats' of those who persecuted the Christians was little more than an acknowledgement that in fact these threats did not pass unnoticed by Him. We may hope that the vengeful cry which characterises some of the Psalms is not echoed here, but rather that something of the Lord's forgiveness of His murderers has been learnt. The reference at least is brief – 'O Lord, mark their threats', and the prayer passes on to an urgent request for grace to continue to 'speak Thy word with all boldness' – a request no sooner made than it was granted (v. 31).

With that prayer for boldness of speech went a plea that the power of God, through the Person of Christ, might be seen in the healing of the sick. Stories in The Acts and references in the Epistles indicate that the prayer was answered. The story of the Church has been an interesting commentary on the fact that, when God's servants have been humble enough to be His agents and prayerful enough to pray as did this group in Acts 4, the healing work has been continued – 'signs and wonders' have been done 'through the name of Thy holy servant Jesus'.

Acts 7: 59

A.V.	N.E.B.
59. Lord Jesus, receive my spirit.	'Lord Jesus, receive my spirit.'

There is no hint in the Gospels that Stephen was near to the cross when Jesus was crucified. Conceivably he may have been. We shall never know. But it is certain that, even if he were not, he would often have heard from the first Christians detailed accounts of how Jesus had died. In these accounts he would have learned how the last prayer of Jesus was one of committal, 'Father, into Thy hands I commend My spirit' (*St. Luke* 23: 46; see pp. 55 ff.). On these words he must frequently have pondered.

And then, his turn came. Death by stoning was an ugly death; not as bad as crucifixion, but bad enough – slow, excruciating, bloody. The writer of the story describes the scene vividly – the ferocity of the conscience-stricken crowd (vv. 54, 57-58), the composure of the Spirit-filled proto-martyr (v. 55), the presence of the ascended Christ standing ready to succour him (vv. 55-56). 'It is enough for the disciple that he be as his master'. The Master had prayed: 'Into Thy hands I commend My spirit'. The disciple prayed: 'Receive my spirit'. He had learned from the Lord the lesson of how to die.

But while there is a close similarity between the prayers, there is also a striking difference. Jesus addressed His prayer to the

'Father'. Stephen addressed his prayer to the 'Lord Jesus'. This is very remarkable. Only the briefest period of time had passed since Jesus moved among men in the flesh. But already we find prayer being addressed to Him – and that on the part of one who presumably was a rigid monotheist. He catches a vision of Jesus, ascended and glorified, and it seems only natural to address prayer to Him. It was a long time before the Creeds were to be hammered out or the great Church Councils held. But Christolatry preceded Christology – prayer came before the definition of doctrine.

Acts 7: 60

A.V.

N.E.B.

60. Lord, lay not this sin to their charge.

'Lord, do not hold this sin against them.'

Again in this prayer, as in the prayer of the previous verse, we hear a clear echo of one of our Lord's prayers on the cross: 'Father, forgive them; for they know not what they do' (*St. Luke* 23: 34; see pp. 53 ff.). Did Stephen know the Lord's Prayer, with its searching clause, 'Forgive us our debts, as we forgive our debtors' (*St. Matthew* 6: 12 and *St. Luke* 11: 4; see pp. 33 ff.)? It is more than likely that he did, and that he had begun to glimpse how mighty and creative a thing forgiveness is.

But even he could little guess the effect which his death, and his forgiveness in the act of dying, would have on one who was standing by, and so on the whole history of the Christian Church. 'Saul was among those who approved of his murder' (8: 1, N.E.B.); and he had been standing by, taking his part, even if a passive one, by looking after the coats of those who did the actual stoning (7: 58). 'If Stephen had not prayed, the Church would not have had Paul' – Augustine was right. We think of the conversion of St. Paul as being a sudden one – indeed, it is often taken as the classic example of such conversions. But this is only very partially true. Adolf Deissmann pointed out that there was much inflammable material on which the lightning of Damascus was to strike. Stephen provided much of that material. What happened in Saul's experience between the day when Stephen died and the day when the light shone on the Damascus road? Young Saul, outwardly so confident, so blusteringly efficient in his persecution of the followers of the Way, had many a night of misery between those days of hectic activity. The face of Stephen – how could he ever forget it? The voice of Stephen, calling on his Lord to receive his spirit and forgive his murderers, rang in his ears sleepless night after sleepless night, until at last he capitulated to the love of God in Christ.

As the Lord, going to His death, had turned and looked on Peter in forgiving love, and, breaking him, had begun to remake him, so the forgiving love of the Church's first martyr broke Saul's opposition, and had a large part in giving to the Church its greatest apostle to the Gentiles.

Acts 9: 5

A.V.	N.E.B.
5. Who art thou, Lord?	'Tell me, Lord, . . . who you are.'

Acts 9: 6

A.V.	
6. Lord, what wilt thou have me to do?	[Omitted in N.E.B.]

Acts 22: 10

A.V.	N.E.B.
10. What shall I do, Lord?	'What shall I do, Lord?'

There are three accounts of the conversion of St. Paul in the Acts of the Apostles — the first, the historian's straightforward story (9: 1 ff.), the second St. Paul's account at Jerusalem (22: 1 ff.), the third his account at Caesarea before King Agrippa (26: 2 ff.). All these accounts include his question-prayer, 'Who art Thou, Lord?' (9: 5; 22: 8; 26: 15). The last account omits the prayer, 'Lord, what wilt Thou have me to do?' The account in chapter 22 has it (v. 10, in the form 'What shall I do, Lord?'), and the historian's own account has it, but only in some inferior manuscripts, in the form 'Lord, what wilt Thou have me to do?' (This question is given in the Authorised Version, but omitted in the Revised Version and in the New English Bible.) Since both questions occur, fully attested, in one of the accounts, we shall consider both here. They are too closely related to be considered separately.

Prayer in question form is prayer in one of its best forms, for prayer is a seeking after God, His nature and His will. This is dialogue – the asking of questions, and the listening for an answer. The child, ignorant and groping, seeks the mind of the Father. This is the reverse of the child dictating to the Father – which is a travesty of prayer. The man who prays is content to ask questions – 'Who . . . ?' 'What . . . ?' – and is not impatient if the answer is delayed or if it comes but slowly and partially. 'Here we see through a glass, darkly . . .' but as we continue to ask our questions, persistently and humbly, we shall be allowed to see more, here a little, there a little, and one day 'face to face'.

The Psalms are full of questions, sometimes meditatively addressed by the Psalmist to himself, 'Why art thou cast down, O my soul . . . ?' (42: 5), sometimes addressed to God, 'My God, my God, why hast Thou forsaken me . . . ?' (22: 1), 'Lord, how long shall the wicked . . . triumph?' (94: 3), 'Lord, what is man, that Thou hast such respect unto him . . . ?' (144: 3, P.B.V.), and so on. There is a questioning which is not rebellion, but is honest seeking after God; and we may believe that God delights to hear and to answer such prayer.

The question, 'Who art Thou, Lord?' is the most important question a man can ask. To face the problem of the Person of Christ is to face the most urgent question in the world. It was this question with which Jesus confronted His disciples, turning an interesting discussion into a personal challenge to faith (*St. Matthew*, 16: 13 ff., 'Some say . . . But whom say ye . . . ?') and eliciting St. Peter's tremendous answer, 'Thou art the Christ, the Son of the living God'. It was on this point that our Lord's rebuke to Philip turned: 'Have I been all this time with you, Philip, and you still do not *know Me*?' (*St. John* 14: 9, N.E.B.).

The editors of a recent book on the thought of F. D. Maurice, in a section headed 'Maurice as a Man in Christ', write: 'He considered Christ both the Word which confronted him and the Person at work in his life, actually giving him all sympathy with others, all strength in temptation, all true thought of good intention. These things, he believed, were first found in Christ, then distributed to men. Christ gave each individual and all mankind truth and righteousness. The Christian life was trust and nothing but trust; yet the trust produced certain fruits . . . all that Paul calls the fruit of the Spirit' (*Toward the Recovery of Unity*, edited by John F. Porter and William J. Wolf, p. 19). 'With Maurice', they write, 'Christology furnishes in a unique way the underlying principle for all that he said and did . . . He saw the unifying power of Christology more clearly, perhaps, than any other Christian thinker' (p. 21). In the light of this, we can understand Maurice's complaint: '. . . We have been dosing our people with religion when what they want is not this but the Living God' (p. 24). For him, *the* question was: 'Who art Thou, Lord?'

The word 'Lord' can in itself mean little or much. *Kurios* is a word used by an inferior to a superior — that is about all that can be said of it in itself. It takes its full meaning from its context. Sometimes it means 'Sir'; sometimes — very frequently in the Greek version of the Old Testament — it is used of God Almighty. What content was Saul to put into it that day on the Damascus Road? That was the nub of the question. Soon he was to see; and the answer is worked out in the letters he was later to write.

The reply is full of interest: 'I am Jesus, whom you are persecuting'. It is interesting for how *little* it says. The Lord began *where Saul was*. Jesus — that is how he knew about Him (even if he had not personally known Him). But it is interesting also for how *much* it implies — 'Jesus, whom you are persecuting'. 'But, Lord', we can imagine him objecting, 'I am not persecuting You; I am persecuting Your followers'. And the reply dawned on him: 'You cannot do one without doing the other. Persecute them and you persecute Me. There is an indivisible unity between disciples and Master' (cf. *St. Mathews* 25: 40, 45). Was it *here* that St. Paul's doctrine of the Church, with its unity of Head and members, began?

There followed the second question-prayer: 'Lord, what am I to do? What do You want me to do?' At once, the will sprang into action. 'I was not disobedient to the heavenly vision', he was later to tell King Agrippa (26: 19). Christology alone could conceivably remain simply a theological exercise — but not when the question 'Who art Thou, Lord?' was asked in earnest prayer, as was the case with Saul. The Person of Christ, the obedience of the will — these pregnant question-prayers were not left unanswered — 'Get up and go into the city, and you will be told what you have to do' (9: 6). A step at a time. Stop praying. Act.

So the persecutor launched out into his life of apostleship.

Acts 9: 10

A.V.   N.E.B.

10. Behold, I am here, Lord.   'Here I am, Lord.'

Acts 9: 13-14

A.V.

13. Lord, I have heard by many of this man, how much evil he hath done to thy saints at Jerusalem:

14. And here he hath authority from the chief priests to bind all that call on thy name.

N.E.B.

'Lord, I have often heard about this man and all the harm he has done to thy people in Jerusalem.

And here he is with authority from the chief priests to arrest all who invoke thy name.'

On the face of it, this does not appear to be a very edifying display of prayer! But it is not to be neglected. At least two points call for comment:

i. The divine call comes — 'Ananias!' And swiftly the answer comes back: 'Here I am, Lord' (v. 10, N.E.B.). Ready — listening — at attention! This is the true spirit of prayer. It is the spirit in which the disciple stands

> 'Alert and quick to hear
> Each whisper of Thy call'.

This 'waiting attitude of expectation' is worth far more than a spate of words. It is hinted at in the instructions given by our Lord in regard to prayer — 'enter into thine inner chamber, and *having shut thy door*, pray . . .' (*St. Matthew* 6: 6, R.V.). There is preparation called for before real prayer can begin. There is a spirit of recollection to be gained. Without this, a period of prayer, or the saying of the Offices, can only too easily become vain repetition.

> 'This sanctuary of my soul
> Unwitting I keep white and whole,
> Unlatched and lit, if Thou shouldst care
> To enter or to tarry there.
>
> With parted lips and outstretched hands
> And listening ears, Thy servant stands,
> Call Thou early, call Thou late,
> To Thy great service dedicate.'
>
> (Charles Hamilton Sorley, *Expectans Expectavi*)

ii. The rest of the prayer (vv. 13-14) is an objection raised by Ananias to God. 'But this is impossible! Send me to Saul? The man is in hot pursuit of people like myself! What an errand!' The objection was overruled (vv. 15-16), and Ananias went (v.17) and did his work with the utmost graciousness. It took some divine charity to lay his hands on Saul's head, and address him as '*Brother Saul*'. That act of sheer grace may well have been the last link in the conversion of the erstwhile persecutor.

Was Ananias to be blamed for objecting? Perhaps so. The strictest among us would say that he should have gone, and asked no questions. 'He that is without sin among you, let him first cast a stone'! But Ananias was honest and open with God. Is not that a primary requirement in prayer?

Certainly when we turn to the Psalms, the element of complaint is a considerable one. 'Awake, why sleepest Thou?' (44: 23); 'Hast not Thou forsaken us, O God?' (108: 11, P.B.V.); the list could be continued without difficulty. And the saints down the ages have not been ashamed to complain – did not St. Teresa tell the Almighty that it was small wonder He had so few friends if He treated them all as He was treating her?

'I will complain in the bitterness of my soul' (*Job* 7: 11). 'Job the blasphemer was far more deeply religious than any of his orthodox friends' – Paul Scherer makes the point (*The Word God Sent*, pp. 56-57). Later in the book, he writes of John the Baptist and the question wrung from him in prison, 'Art Thou He that should come, or do we look for another?': '. . . in one of the most touching scenes of the New Testament (Jesus) sprang to John's defense. I suppose the elders and the scribes were snickering in their beards. The herald was not making out so well with his heralding any more! He had been so sure. He had flayed them alive with his tongue. There seemed to be a few misgivings now, and a good thing it was! But Jesus would have none of it. He looked around the circle. Full in their teeth He flung it at them: "You think he was a reed shaken by the wind? Or a softling, like the fops who dawdle hours away in kings' houses? I tell you he was a prophet. No man was ever greater than he!"' (p. 63).

Dr. Frank Lake, in his *Clinical Theology*, tells how he came upon a letter written by the saintly Robert Leighton, Archbishop of Glasgow, to a woman suffering from depression. 'As a father pities his child when it is sick, and in the rage and reveries of a fever, though it even utter reproachful words against himself, shall not our dearest Father both forgive and pity those thoughts in any child of His, that arise not from any wilful hatred of Him, but are kindled in hell within them? . . . When these assaults come thickest and violentest upon you, throw yourself down at His footstool and

say O God, Father of mercies, save me from this hell within me . . .
Thus, *or in whatever frame your soul shall be carried to vent itself
into His bosom*, be sure your words, yea your silent sighs and
breathings shall not be lost . . .' (p. 369).

'I will complain.' The Father will understand.

Acts 10: 14

A.V.	N.E.B.
14. Not so, Lord; for I have never eaten anything that is common or unclean.	'No, Lord, no: I have never eaten anything profane or unclean.'

This is not a hesitation or objection, as was Ananias' prayer (9:
13-14). This is a flat 'No' — a refusal. 'No, Lord, no; I have never
eaten anything profane or unclean' (N.E.B.). If this had been a
case of straightforward prayer, we should be entitled to say that
this was sin — no man has a right to say 'No' to God. But, in fact,
we are dealing with the story of a man in a trance, a strange kind of
dream, with 'a thing coming down that looked like a great sheet of
sail-cloth . . . creatures of every kind . . . a voice . . .' (vv. 11-13,
N.E.B.). It has about it all the marks of those dreams which harass
and distress.

Yet to St. Peter, as to so many of the Biblical figures, a trance
brought a message very clear in its implications — terrifyingly clear
in the light of immediately subsequent events. The rest of the
chapter is given up to the story of how St. Peter was led to see that
the old distinction between Jew and Gentile was no longer relevant
— was, indeed, contrary to the mind of God. What God counted
clean he was not to call profane. St. Paul was to have occasion, as
he graphically tells us in *Galatians* 2: 11 ff., to rebuke St. Peter to
his face, because, after taking his meals with Gentiles, he drew
back and began to hold aloof out of fear of some people newly
arrived from Jerusalem. But that was only a temporary lapse. The
trance which brought him such utter revulsion that he found
himself saying 'No, Lord, no . . .', was followed by costly
obedience, and St. Peter found his old, sincerely held inhibitions
giving way to the charity of the Gospel.

What has this moving story to say to us in an age when God is
calling us to lower our barriers in the interests of a truly ecumenical
love?

86

THE PRAYERS IN THE LETTERS

IF we look in the writings of St. Paul for a full enunciation of his 'philosophy' of prayer, his 'theory' of prayer, we shall be disappointed. We shall not find it. The Apostle is not, in the main, concerned to lecture to his converts about prayer. Rather, he gives us a glimpse or two of his own experiences of prayer, various exhortations to pray, and one passage (*Romans* 8: 26-27) in which he briefly expounds the theology of prayer. He has good precedent for such a procedure. Jesus, so the Gospels would seem to indicate, was not at pains to lecture to His disciples about God. Rather, He encouraged them to share with Him His own experience of God as Father and as King. All that He taught about God's paternal governance sprang from His own experience of God in His life. *That*, immensely alive, deep, relevant to His hearers, was the *fons et origo* of all His teaching. As with the Master, so with the Apostle. His own experience of God in Christ, his own experience of prayer, was the soil out of which his prayer-life grew. This he shared with his hearers and readers, partly by telling them what in fact he prayed for them, partly by autobiographical hints, partly by exhortation.

At this point, a word must be said about his own background. We have already had occasion to point out the influence of the prayer of St. Stephen on the conversion of Saul of Tarsus (*Acts* 7: 60; see pp. 80 ff.). But is it not more than probable that Saul was himself, as it were, conceived and born in prayer? Of his parents we know but little. We know of his father's Roman citizenship (*Acts* 22: 28). We know of his parents' orthodox Judaism—he describes himself as 'a Hebrew born and bred' (*Philippians* 3: 5, N.E.B.). Behind that phrase within its context we can well imagine a strict and godly home, and the growing boy surrounded by the prayers of his religious father and mother. Probably those prayers were answered 'above all that they asked or thought'—to their dismay, when they saw their son forsake his persecution of the Nazarene and follow Him with all his mind and strength. He refers (*Philippians* 3: 8) to having 'suffered the loss of all things'. This phrase may reflect a painful scene when he was turned out of his home because of his 'unorthodoxy'. God sometimes has a way of surprising us in answering our prayers in ways far other than what we imagined! We can do little more than surmise here, for the material on which we have to work is very small indeed.

We are on firmer ground when we come to consider the vocabulary which St. Paul uses when he writes of the Christian's relationship with God in Christ, a relationship entered into and realised in prayer. Let us take an example. Three times in his epistles he uses a word (*prosagōgē*) which the Authorised Version, with no very great imagination, translates 'access'. The references, which are worthy of close study, are Ephesians 2: 18; 3: 12, and Romans 5: 2. The New English Bible translates the first two occurrences of the word by 'access' and the last by a periphrasis – 'we have been allowed to enter the sphere (of God's grace)'. The word indicates a way into the courts of the presence chamber of God. The verb from which the noun is derived occurs in 1 *Peter* 3: 18 – 'Christ also hath once suffered for sins . . . that He might *bring* us *to* God'. Commenting on the verb, James Denney wrote: 'The word . . . has always a touch of formality in it; it is a great occasion when the Son Who has assumed our responsibilities for us takes us by the hand to bring us to the Father . . . Sin . . . keeps man at a distance from God; but Christ has so dealt with sin on man's behalf that its separative force is annulled' (*The Death of Christ*, pp. 102 and 103, fifth edition, 1905).

'It is through Him' writes the Apostle (*Ephesians* 2: 18) 'that we both' (i.e. Jews and Gentiles together) 'have (our) *introduction* through one Spirit to the Father'. *Introduction* – so Meyer would translate the word when it occurs in *Romans* 5: 2, and Ellicott in this occurrence in Ephesians. 'In Him we have our boldness and introduction with confidence through faith in Him' (*Ephesians* 3: 12). By a construction which the grammarians call *hendiadys*, this virtually means 'the boldness of our introduction', or 'our bold introduction'. Or, as other commentators take the word: 'We have our *approach*' (cf. *Romans* 5: 2). Moulton and Milligan have a delightful note (in their *The Vocabulary of the Greek Testament*, s.v. *prosagōgē*) in which they hint that the word sometimes means 'a landing stage'. This would agree with Pallis (on *Romans* 5: 2) who thinks that 'grace' in that verse is there pictured as a haven, and that *prosagōgē* means 'approach' in a nautical sense. Thus we have in Ephesians the idea of introduction or approach into the royal presence of God, and in Romans the concept of our approach into the haven where God is and where we in Christ stand. This regal-nautical metaphor is a rich one. Here is the union of faith, enjoyed and entered into in prayer.

Nor, for all St. Paul's sense of the numinous and of the awe-full, is this access enjoyed 'with trembling hope', as one of our hymns has it. Rather, it is entered into with 'boldness' — the suggestion is that the Christian's hope is a tingling rather than a trembling one. For the presence into which we consciously enter in prayer is the presence of One who has disclosed Himself as our Father.

This leads us to consider another passage which is highly relevant to St. Paul's conception of prayer. I refer to *Romans* 8: 14-17. (There is a similar, though slightly shorter, passage in *Galatians* 4: 6-7.) The theme is that of sonship of God and its bearing on prayer. The verses open with the searching remark that those are sons of God who in fact are *led* by the Spirit of God — 'moved', says the New English Bible. (The word is identical with that used of the Son of God being *driven* by the Spirit of God, in *St. Luke* 4: 1.) Then the Apostle looks back to the day of his readers' baptism — so the aorist tenses would suggest. What happened on that great day? The answer is given, first, in negative terms — 'You did *not* receive a spirit of slavery such as would lead you to relapse into the state of fear which you knew in the old days'. Then, in positive terms — 'on the contrary, you *did* receive a Spirit of adoption, a Spirit that makes us sons, a Spirit that enables us to cry out "Abba! Father!"' It is interesting to notice that St. Paul, though writing in Greek to those accustomed to speak and read Greek, retains the Aramaic word 'Abba', a word so little known to his readers that he has to translate it into Greek — '*pater*', 'father'. He retains it (as he does also in the parallel passage in Galatians) because it was the very word which so often fell from the lips of Jesus when He prayed, and therefore was a very precious part of the heritage of the Church (see pp. 20-21). It is tempting to think that in this passage we have a reference to the very first post-baptismal act of the Christian converts. They laid aside their old garments. They went down into the water — were, indeed, 'buried with Christ' — they came up into newness of life. They put on their white robes. And, exultantly, triumphantly, as members of the Body of Christ, they 'cried out "Abba! Father"'. Their longing was that His Kingdom should come and His will be done in earth as it is in heaven.

Within them as they prayed was the witness of the Spirit (v. 16, *testimonium internum Spiritus sancti*) — 'children of God, heirs of God, joint-heirs with Christ', fellow-sufferers with Him, heirs of glory with Him.

In studying this great passage, we are very near to the beginnings of the Christian Church – we can sense something of its pulsating life and deep joy. And we are close to the core of St. Paul's experience of prayer – 'Abba! Father!' Prayer took him, indeed, into the audience-chamber of the King. But that King was also Father. Prayer took him into the intimacy of filial communion with Him. We shall never understand the prayers of St. Paul if we forget that this concept governs them all.

There is a passage of great poignancy in one of his letters in which, under a faintly disguised anonymity, St. Paul allows us to see into one of the hardest lessons which he had to learn in the school of life and of prayer. I refer to 2 *Corinthians* 12: 1-10. He tells the story in the third person, rather than in the first, but there can be little doubt that it is of his own experience that he is writing. All seemed to be going well with this 'Christian man' (v. 2, N.E.B.). There were visions. There were revelations. There was great elation. And then it came – something as ugly and as painful as the Greek word which is used to describe it, *skolops*, a stake, something sharp which pierces and makes one bleed. Was it physical? – epilepsy, eye-trouble, some mischievous germ picked up in a malaria-infested region of his travels? The New English Bible would indicate that it was – 'a sharp pain in my body' (v. 7). That is a free translation, but it may be right; 'flesh' may well mean here just what it says, and not some other sphere of anguish. His reaction to this 'pain' was the right one. He betook himself to prayer about it, not on one occasion only but thrice. 'Lord', he prayed, 'rid me of it.' We can almost overhear him proffering his reasons why he should be freed of it – 'it hinders my work; it curtails my activities; it holds up the proclamation of the Gospel'.

God answered His servant's prayers. He always does. In this instance, He answered with a quite firm negative. 'No, my son, no. You must learn to live with it. There is no way *out* of this. I will see you *through* it. I will be with you *in* it. And *in* the weakness and the agony you will learn a lesson that you cannot well learn out of it. You will learn the sufficiency of the grace of God and the over-shadowing power of Christ.' Who is to say that his life and ministry were not infinitely enriched by that experience of pain triumphed over in prayer?

In 1941 Edward Woods, then Bishop of Lichfield, gave a series of broadcasts entitled *Things I Live By*. In the last of them, a talk called *Chastening Accepted*, he did as St. Paul did, and spoke of his own experience in the third person: 'I know a man who, some time ago, had a serious breakdown in health and was obliged to go abroad for some years. It meant the break-up of his home, the abandonment of useful and interesting work, and the future looked black. On the Channel crossing he found running in his head the title of one of Tolstoy's tales, "Things Men Live By"; and he wondered if his present disaster was one of the things he had to learn to live by. In the event he found that it was so. The thing took indeed a lot of learning, and there were some kicks against the pricks; but the time did come when he could honestly thank God for what had at first seemed sheer calamity' (*The Life of Edward Woods*, by Oliver Tomkins, p. 35).

It is small wonder that, as a result of rich lessons learned through the 'sharp pain', St. Paul wrote to the Thessalonians (1 *Thessalonians* 5: 17): 'Never give up prayer' (Moffatt), and to the Ephesians: 'Give yourselves wholly to prayer and entreaty; pray on every occasion in the power of the Spirit', adding, for he knew how many lessons awaited the man of prayer, 'to this end keep watch and persevere' (*Ephesians* 6: 18, N.E.B.). All too easily the lessons could be missed.

Finally, we come to that passage which, in the opening paragraph of the chapter, I described as the one in which he briefly expounds the theology of prayer — *Romans* 8: 26-27. Earlier in this chapter, as we have seen, he referred to that Spirit which enables us to cry out 'Abba! Father!' (v. 15). Now he returns to the subject. When a man engages in prayer, he is not alone. Heiler was right when he wrote — and St. Paul would have corroborated his statement — 'Prayer is not man's work or discovery or achievement, but God's work in man' (*Prayer*, p. iv). There is one who *comes to the aid* of his weakness. The word so translated occurs only once elsewhere in the Greek New Testament. It is in the passage where Martha, busy in the kitchen, suggests to Jesus that He should bid the devoted Mary '*lend her a hand*' with the work of preparing the meal (*St. Luke* 10: 40, N.E.B.). The Spirit, says the Apostle, lends us a hand, takes an interest in us, when we are at the work of prayer. We do not toil alone.

This throws light on the ensuing sentences. 'We do not know how to pray as we ought' (v. 26, R.S.V.). That is obvious enough. 'Our ignorance in asking' (as one of the post-Communion collects puts it) is a reality which anyone who tries to pray knows a good deal about. The 'things which for our unworthiness we dare not and for our blindness we cannot ask' are legion. Do we despair, then, of the whole enterprise? Not at all. Luther got to the heart of the matter when, with his usual forthrightness, he wrote: 'All that the man, or the spirit in him, can manage is a little sound and a feeble groaning as "Ah! Father", and the Father understands – a simple vocative without expression and connection is established'. That is well said. An infant can only cry, wordlessly, but the mother understands. The man or woman at prayer, so deep is their longing and so great their ignorance, can only emit a groan. But the Spirit intercedes, and the Father understands, and forces are set in motion of which the world knows nothing.

This, surely, is the meaning of the words translated in the Authorised Version and Revised Version 'with groanings which cannot be uttered'. Anders Nygren, in his *Commentary on Romans* (pp. 330-331) wrote: 'Paul speaks in this section about a threefold groaning: (1) the whole creation groans (vv. 19-22); (2) the Christian groans (vv. 23-25); and (3) the Spirit himself groans (vv. 26-27)'. But surely the New English Bible is correct in translating, though slightly freely, 'through our inarticulate groans'. It is we who groan, because of our ignorance and short-sightedness and narrow-mindedness. It is He, the gracious Spirit, who, at the point of our deepest need, interprets our groanings to the Father, in this, as in everything, co-operating for good with those who love God (v. 28, N.E.B.).

No need, then, to abandon prayer, just because we are weak or ignorant. Here, as in every department of Christian life and activity, we have, in Binney's words,

> 'a Holy Spirit's energies,
> An Advocate with God'.

C. S. Lewis touches on this in his *Letters to Malcolm Chiefly on Prayer* (pp. 92 ff.). 'If the Holy Spirit speaks in the man, then in prayer God speaks to God.' He quotes a poem 'found in an old notebook . . . with no author's name attached' (I wonder – was the name C. S. Lewis?[1]):

> 'They tell me, Lord, that when I seem
> To be in speech with you,
> Since but one voice is heard, it's all a dream,
> One talker aping two.

[1] My guess was right. Since I first wrote this, a book of C. S. Lewis' *Poems*, edited by Walter Hooper, has been published, and this poem is included in a slightly altered form (pp. 122-3. Geoffrey Bles, 1964). In this same book, he ends another poem, 'Footnote to all prayers', with this couplet which again comes very close to St. Paul:
> Take not, oh Lord, our literal sense. Lord, in Thy great,
> Unbroken speech our limping metaphor translate. (p. 129.)

Sometimes it is, yet not as they
    Conceive it. Rather, I
Seek in myself the things I hoped to say,
    But lo!, my wells are dry.

Then, seeing me empty, you forsake
    The listener's role and through
My dumb lips breathe and into utterance wake
    The thoughts I never knew.

And thus you neither need reply
    Nor can; thus, while we seem
Two talkers, thou art One forever, and I
    No dreamer, but thy dream.'

Lewis then proceeds to quarrel with the word *dream* as suggesting Pantheism and adds: 'But is he not right in thinking that prayer in its most perfect state is a soliloquy?' Lewis is not far from St. Paul here.

BEGINNINGS AND ENDINGS—A NOTE

Most of the Pauline letters — and indeed most of the others in the New Testament — begin with a greeting which is really a brief prayer and end with another. There is an element of sameness and an element of variety about these beginnings and endings. They are worthy of study. We shall take an over-all look at them here:

Beginnings

The form 'Grace to you, and peace, from God our Father and the Lord Jesus Christ' is found in almost exactly the same words in *Romans* 1 : 7; 1 *Corinthians* 1 : 3; 2 *Corinthians* 1 : 2; *Galatians* 1 : 3 (with an important addition in vv. 4-5); *Ephesians* 1 : 2; *Philippians* 1 : 2; 2 *Thessalonians* 1 : 2; *Philemon* 3. In *Colossians* 1 : 2 the words 'and the Lord Jesus Christ' and in 1 *Thessalonians* 1 : 1 the words 'from God our Father and the Lord Jesus Christ' are omitted in important manuscripts. In 1 *Timothy* 1 : 2 and 2 *Timothy* 1 : 2 the form varies — 'grace, mercy, and peace from God the Father and Christ Jesus (or, Jesus Christ) our Lord'; in *Titus* 1 : 4 it is 'grace (mercy), and peace, from God the Father and (the Lord) Jesus Christ our Saviour'.

Outside the letters which bear the name of St. Paul, there is little to add. *James* 1 : 1 has the brief word 'greeting'. 1 *Peter* 1 : 2

has 'grace to you, and peace be multiplied'. *Jude* (v. 2) has 'mercy unto you, and peace, and love, be multiplied'.

We shall comment on the initial greeting as it occurs in *Romans* 1: 7, and in the other cases simply give a cross-reference back, except in the case of the Pastoral Epistles where a special note is called for on 1 *Timothy* 1: 2.

Endings

There are a few endings to the New Testament letters which are really ascriptions. The longest, which is almost creedal in form and in a sense is recapitulatory of the main message of the Epistle, is that of the Epistle to the Romans (16: 25-27). The others are 2 *Peter* 3: 18 and *Jude* 24-25.

The full 'Trinitarian' form of what has come to be known as 'the Grace' occurs only in 2 *Corinthians* 13: 14 – 'the grace of the Lord Jesus Christ, and the love of God, and the communion of the Holy Ghost, be with you all'. The other endings are mostly variants on the first phrase of this prayer. Sometimes it is simply 'Grace be with you (all)', or, 'with thee', as in *Colossians* 4: 18; 1 *Timothy* 6: 21; *Titus* 3: 15; *Hebrews* 13: 25. Sometimes this is made more explicit – 'The grace of the (our) Lord Jesus Christ be with you (all; your spirit; your spirit, brethren)', as in *Romans* 16: 24 (in some manuscripts); 1 *Corinthians* 16: 23 (where this is prefaced by *Marana tha*, and followed by 'My love be with you all in Christ Jesus, Amen'); *Galatians* 6: 18; *Philippians* 4: 23; 1 *Thessalonians* 5: 28; 2 *Thessalonians* 3: 18, and *Philemon* 25. In *Ephesians* 6: 24, this blessing is slightly elaborated – 'grace be with all them that love our Lord Jesus Christ in sincerity', or, according to the New English Bible, 'God's grace be with all who love our Lord Jesus Christ, grace and immortality'. 2 *Timothy* 4: 22 has 'The Lord Jesus Christ be with thy spirit. Grace be with you', while two Epistles strike the note of *peace* which, we have noticed, occurs in almost all the initial greetings of the New Testament letters (1 *Peter* 5: 14, 'Peace be with you all that are in Christ Jesus'; and 3 *John* 14, 'Peace be to thee').

Apart, therefore, from the ascriptions and from those few additions which call for notes, we shall comment on the full form of the *Grace* as it occurs in 2 *Corinthians* 13: 14, and in other instances content ourselves with a cross-reference back to it.

THE EPISTLE TO THE ROMANS

Romans 1: 7

A.V.	N.E.B.
7. Grace to you and peace from God our Father, and the Lord Jesus Christ.	Grace and peace to you from God our Father and the Lord Jesus Christ.

WE have already noticed, in commenting on Stephen's prayer in *Acts* 7: 59 – 'Lord Jesus, receive my spirit' – that it came naturally to the very early Christians, when they prayed, to address their prayers to the Lord Jesus. When they knelt down and looked up into the Face of God, they saw, as it were, the lineaments of the Lord Jesus. It took a man of the stature of the Seer of the Apocalypse to be able to write down the vision granted to him, and to describe 'in the midst of the throne . . . a Lamb standing' with the marks of the passion on Him (*Revelation* 5: 6). But long before he wrote, Christians were addressing their prayers to that Lamb slain and triumphant. And very early in the history of the Christian Church, St. Paul was greeting his readers jointly 'from God our Father *and* from the Lord Jesus Christ'.

The 'conjunction' of Father and Son, or, as in 'The Grace', of Father, Son and Holy Spirit saved the early Church from degenerating in its praying into what has been called 'Jesus worship', and laid the basis for the fully developed Trinitarianism of subsequent ages.

On *grace*, see 2 *Corinthians* 13: 14; and pp. 117 ff. Here it need only be said that it is frequently connected, in New Testament usage, with the idea of forgiveness. The order of the words, 'grace and peace', in this greeting may, therefore, be significant. There can be no peace where grace has not been operative. First forgiveness: then peace.

What, then, is the Biblical meaning of *peace*, that constantly recurring word in both Testaments?

It is, of course, frequently used of the end of hostilities, as, for example, when two nations who have been at war cease their fighting and live side by side in tranquillity. This idea is taken over in the language of religion. Man by his disobedience is in a state of enmity towards God. He has rebelled. He is at war. Until he is prepared to lay down the arms of his rebellion, there can be no peace, greatly though God longs for it.

Such a state of war leads also to hostility towards his fellow human-beings. It may take the form of class-warfare, or of colour-warfare, or of other kinds of group antipathy. It may take the form of individual spite or jealousy or resentment. This may break out in open violence, or it may smoulder like an underground fire.

A man's wrong relationship with God and his wrong relationship with his neighbour are closely connected. They can be represented by a triangle, at the apex of which is God, the individual being at one other corner and his neighbour at the third. Let us call the individual A. If A is in wrong relationship with his neighbour (be that neighbour his wife or the coloured man down the street), 'automatically' his relationship with God is affected. Again, if A is in wrong relationship with God, his relationship with his neighbour is bound to be affected, for he is living a life crippled by his broken fellowship with God. There can be no peace under such conditions.

The classic New Testament passage which expounds this truth is the second chapter of the Epistle to the Ephesians. Here a double enmity, a double estrangement, is exposed – an estrangement between God and man and between Jew and Gentile. But Christ 'is our peace', reconciling Jew and Gentile in a single body to God (v. 14) – a foretaste of that restoration of the whole creation which is God's great plan for it.

So, in Biblical language, peace is much more than a mere cessation of hostilities, fundamental as that concept is. Peace is, in the words of Pedersen, 'the untrammelled, free growth of the soul (i.e. person) . . . harmonious community'. It is that condition which men enjoy who are in right relationship with one another through the God of peace. 'There is no peace', there can be no peace, 'to the wicked' (*Isaiah* 57: 21).

To give the greeting '. . . peace from God our Father and the Lord Jesus Christ' is, then, to pray that those to whom the greeting is sent may be in such relationship with God and with one another that 'wholeness' may be theirs, health of mind and body and spirit, holiness abundant and infectious.

Romans 1: 8-10

A.V.	N.E.B.
8. First, I thank my God through Jesus Christ for you all, that your faith is spoken of throughout the whole world.	Let me begin by thanking my God, through Jesus Christ, for you all, because all over the world they are telling the story of your faith.
9. For God is my witness, whom I serve with my spirit in the gospel of his Son, that without ceasing I make mention of you always in my prayers;	God is my witness, the God to whom I offer the humble service of my spirit by preaching the gospel of his Son:
10. Making request, if by any means now at length I might have a prosperous journey by the will of God to come unto you.	God knows how continually I make mention of you in my prayers, and am always asking that by his will I may, somehow or other, succeed at long last in coming to visit you.

The prayer-greeting of v. 7 is the preface to a passage in which St. Paul does not, indeed, give the exact words of a prayer but rather tells his readers the gist of what happens between him and God when he thinks of them. The section falls into two parts—thanksgiving (v. 8) and petition (vv. 9 ff.).

The order—first thanksgiving, then petition—is one which we shall have occasion to notice again more than once. It may be said to enshrine a principle of the devotional life. The garden of prayer is richer if it has been first watered by thanksgiving.

The cause for the thanksgiving of the apostle is that 'all over the world' the story of the faith of the Roman Christians is being told. Not indeed that he himself had been the one first to evangelise Rome. He had not yet visited the Church there. There is no element of personal pride in this thanksgiving. How precisely the Gospel had first reached Rome we cannot say—presumably it was through a trader here, a soldier there, a slave bearing his witness to his new-found Lord. But it *had* reached Rome; and, as all roads led to Rome and from Rome, those roads had become highways for the Gospel. The news of their faith had sounded out; and to the apostle it was cause for joyful thanksgiving.

So from thanksgiving (v. 8) to petition (vv. 9-10). It was a natural petition on the part of a man who above all else was a pastor. He longed to see the people of whose faith he had heard— 'somehow or other' to visit them.

This introduces us to a phrase which we shall notice elsewhere in St. Paul's writings – 'making mention of you in my prayers' (v. 9 cf. *Ephesians* 1: 16; *Philippians* 1: 3; 1 *Thessalonians* 1: 2; 2 *Timothy* 1: 3; *Philemon* 4.) It is a highly suggestive one. Very often we do not know just *what* we ought to pray for someone in dire need. It is enough, on such occasions, simply to 'make mention' of them in our prayers, to hold them up before God with no word spoken but their names. John Baillie, whose little book *A Diary of Private Prayer* has been not the least of his many gifts to his readers, once said: 'Prayer is, after all, but thinking towards God'. When I make mention in my prayers of someone in need, of someone I love, I think of him towards God. In similar vein, George Macdonald wrote to a friend: 'I will not say that I will pray for you, but I shall think of God and you together'.

This part of prayer – intercessory prayer – calls for method. Memories are unreliable, and anyway they become overcrowded with a multitude of concerns. Some kind of lists will be called for if 'making mention of you in my prayers' is not to become a very haphazard affair. The lists must not be allowed to become tyrants to us, else prayer will become a burden. But they will act as *aides-memoire*, as guides, as reminders.

The burden of St. Paul's prayer, as we have seen (v. 10), was that he might come to see the Roman Christians. This desire is elaborated in v. 11 – he wanted to bring them 'some spiritual gift to make you strong' (N.E.B.). He was a man richly endowed with the gifts of God's grace. He had treasures which he needs must share. He was doing precisely that in all the churches which he visited in his missionary travels – why should the Roman church be excluded? But this was not all. He wanted (v. 12) to be a receiver as well as a giver. He needed the encouragement which they could give him. He must feel the stimulus of their faith on his own, as no doubt his own faith would stimulate theirs when they met face to face and shared the wealth of God's grace.

So he prays – and the prayer is rich in teaching for the modern Church. 'The ministry' is always in danger of becoming over-professionalised. The traffic all too easily becomes one-way. The apostle, the priest, the pastor gives, gives, gives. And it is right that he should. He has been trained for the exercise of a ministry of giving. He has been ordained for this very thing. He draws all his cares and studies this way 'to bring you some spiritual gift to make you strong'. But if his ministry stops there, it will be vastly impoverished. His is also a ministry of receiving. His people are part of the Body of Christ. To them gifts have been given – '*each of us has been given his gift, his due portion of Christ's bounty*' (*Ephesians* 4: 7, N.E.B.). They, in differing degrees, are men of faith. They are not only to be stimulated by the faith of their minister; he is to be stimulated by theirs.

A ministry, therefore, which is one-way is a greatly impoverished ministry. Ways must be sought and found by which real communication, real dialogue, can take place between 'pulpit' and 'pew'. The professor must learn from the shopkeeper, the bishop from the shepherd or farmer or businessman. God has given His gifts of grace and insight not only to the professionally trained.

That this will call for a real measure of humility on the part of the latter there can be no doubt. 'Where is boasting?' Where is professional pride? 'It is excluded.' But that such 'mutuality' as has been described will mean enrichment in depth of fellowship and of Christian joy is equally certain. 'There is an intellectual distance of metres to be traversed between the mind of a layman and that of a clergyman . . . Sometimes this distance exists because the clergyman affects a superiority which he does not possess, or asserts one which he does. In either case, the result is off-putting.' Faithful are the wounds of a friend. The writer is none other than Sir Kenneth Grubb, Chairman of the House of Laity in the Church Assembly (*A Layman Looks at the Church*, pp. 55-6).

We have thought of 'mutuality' between the ordained ministry and the laity in general. But what has been written is particularly true in the matter of preaching. Helmut Thielicke, who fills one of the world's largest churches, St. Michael's in Hamburg, every Sunday with men and women from all walks of life, has recently warned us of the dire peril of 'becoming a church of parsons' – 'there are only a few miserable foot bridges over the chasm between the clergy and the laity . This he blames on the fact that preachers too often neglect the theological-spiritual exchange with laymen which 'is a healing spring for all the problems we face in preaching'. Laymen are in peril of spiritual death because 'they are largely obliged to play the role of a mere "audience", which quite passively allows itself to be homiletically sprinkled' (*The Trouble with the Church: A Call for Renewal*, pp. 28-31). The preacher is not meant to be what Thielicke calls 'a helpless soloist'. He is part of a fellowship, the major part of which is composed of laymen and women, all of them engaged with him in the mutuality of giving and receiving.

Romans 9: 3

A.V.	N.E.B.
3. For I could wish that myself were accursed from Christ for my brethren, my kinsmen according to the flesh.	For I could even pray to be outcast from Christ myself for the sake of my brothers, my natural kinsfolk.

Romans 10: 1

A.V.	N.E.B.
1. Brethren, my heart's desire and prayer to God for Israel is, that they might be saved.	Brothers, my deepest desire and my prayer to God is for their salvation.

It may be objected that these are hardly prayers. Certainly they are of the nature of 'reported speech'; they are indirect. But in 9: 3, the verb is one of the common words for praying. The Authorised Version and Revised Version translate 'I could wish . . .' (R.V. margin, 'pray'). The New English Bible translates 'I could even pray . . .' Perhaps the English idiom 'I had almost caught myself praying' would roughly get what was in the Apostle's mind (cp. C. F. D. Moule — '*I could almost pray to be accursed* — the Imperfect softening the shock of the daring statement or expressing awe at the terrible thought', *An Idiom Book of New Testament Greek*, p. 9). And in 10: 1 the noun 'prayer' is a common word for supplication, request. The verses should not be by-passed.

Here we see the true patriot at the work of prayer, with his patriotism deepened and refined by his Christian faith. By birth and training St. Paul was a Jew. Jewish blood ran in his veins. The roots of his religion and culture ran down deep into Jewish soil. His natural kinsfolk were Israelites, the people who enjoyed a special relationship with the Deity, to whom belonged the covenants, the law, the temple worship, the promises, the patriarchs, and — if they could but see it — the Messiah! But they did not see it, and it seemed they could not see it. There, just there, was the point of agony for St. Paul, the patriot, the Christian patriot. 'I had almost caught myself praying that I myself might be outcast from Christ if that would avail to bring them in.' 'My deepest desire and prayer to God is for their salvation.'

A man does not cease to be a patriot when he becomes a Christian. On the contrary, his patriotism is intensified and purified. If ever he was tempted to think in terms of 'my country right or wrong', he has done with that forever. But the bonds of blood and soil are to him a sacred thing. God has willed him to live and serve against a particular national background. He is a debtor to all the riches which his particular race has gathered, of culture, of art, of science, of music, and so forth. He did not earn these. He inherited them. He is responsible to add to them and to pass them on.

But he also shares in the shame of his race, in the burden of its blindness, its godlessness, its apostasy. And that is where Christian patriotism hurts and costs. 'I could almost pray . . .'

In his agony, the Apostle was in line with many who had gone before him. There is a moving passage in the book of Exodus (ch. 32) in which the passion of Moses for the forgiveness of his people's apostasy is vividly described. He had gone up into the holy mount. The people, in his absence, had inveigled Aaron into making the golden calf. Moses went down from the mount with the tables of the law in his hands. He heard the noise of singing. He saw the calf and the dancing. His anger blazed, and he cast the tables out of his hand, burnt the calf, ground it to powder, scattered it on the water and made the people drink of it. He blazed out against his brother, and wreaked vengeance on the people. Then, the heat of his first anger abated, he turned to the Lord. 'Oh, this people', he said, 'this people have sinned a great sin . . . Yet now, if thou wilt forgive their sin − ; and if not, blot me, I pray thee, out of Thy book which Thou hast written' (vv. 31-32). 'I had almost caught myself praying . . .'

One has only to read the prayer of Ezra (9: 6 ff.) to overhear another patriot at prayer, in agony over the apostasy of his people. One of the most remarkable features of this prayer is the way in which Ezra identified himself with their shame. He did not speak to God of 'their' guilt but of 'ours' − '*I* am ashamed and blush . . . *our* iniquities are increased . . . *our* guiltiness is grown up unto the heavens . . . *we* have forsaken Thy commandments'. 'I had almost caught myself praying . . .' (We may note also the songs in *Lamentations* (e.g. ch. 2, and 3: 48-51) where the poet-prophet laments for Jerusalem in her sin.)

And this, in part, is the meaning of the baptism of Jesus. 'Thus it becometh *us* to fulfil all righteousness' (*St. Matthew* 3: 15). He was one with His brethren, not ashamed to identify Himself with them in the rite of purification, at the lowest point on the earth's surface. So He continued throughout His earthly ministry, till at last He cried 'My God, my God, why hast Thou forsaken Me?' 'I had almost caught myself praying . . .'

Romans 15: 5-6

A.V.	N.E.B.
5. Now the God of patience and consolation grant you to be like-minded one toward another according to Christ Jesus:	And may God, the source of all fortitude and all encouragement, grant that you may agree with one another after the manner of Christ Jesus,
6. That ye may with one mind and one mouth glorify God, even the Father of our Lord Jesus Christ.	So that with one mind and one voice you may praise the God and Father of our Lord Jesus Christ.

Chapter 15 is rich in prayers. There are three – vv. 5-6, v. 13 and v. 33. Each begins with a different description of God, descriptions which in the Revised Version are as follows: 'The God of patience and of comfort' (A.V. 'consolation'); 'the God of hope'; 'the God of peace'. We turn to the first prayer.

'The God of patience and of comfort.' What do these genitives mean ('the God of . . .')? Adolf Deissmann used to call them mystical genitives, and the term is not inapt. Sometimes they almost defy exact and precise definition. Often they are deeply coloured by the context in which they occur. (This is certainly true of the first two of the three prayers in this chapter.) Sometimes there are two or three different shades of meaning, any one of which, or all of which, may be relevant in a particular passage.

In the present instance, the New English Bible translates 'God, *the source of* all fortitude and all encouragement . . .' That is probably the best meaning to attach to the genitives here. Each of the nouns calls for a word of explanation, for each is a word of frequent occurrence and of considerable importance in New Testament vocabulary.

'*Patience*' – so the Authorised and Revised Versions. But 'patience' *can* be a somewhat negative word. 'In spite of great provocation, he exercised remarkable patience', we say. That is, he did not lose his temper; he kept calm. But the New Testament word goes much further and deeper than this. This is steady, positive endurance, the power to *stick it through*, however great the discouragements met with on the way. In this sense it is used, in a

prayer which we shall be considering in 2 *Thessalonians* 3: 5, as a
description of our Lord who, above all others, was an example of
steady endurance throughout His ministry and right to the end. It
is used by St. James (5: 11) of Job. Of all men in the Old Testament, he was the most impatient. Is not the whole poem an
agonised outcry against the current scale of religious values —
against contemporary theology? But Job's *endurance*, his power to
hold on however desperate things became for him — yes, of *this* we
'have heard'.

So the Apostle in this prayer addresses himself to the God who
is the source of this stern kind of stuff of which real Christian
character is made.

But He is more than the source of endurance. He is the source of
comfort (A.V. 'consolation'). Again, these renderings are wholly
inadequate. The New English Bible has *encouragement*, and links
it with the preceding verse in which the Old Testament Scriptures
have been spoken of as a source of encouragement to their readers.
We must look at this word a little more closely. We shall meet it
again.

It is closely connected with the word which is used by St. John,
in chapters 14-16, of the Holy Spirit and once (in 1 *John* 2: 1) of
Jesus Christ. (A.V. and R.V., *Advocate*; R.V. margin, *Comforter*;
N.E.B., *one to plead our cause*.) True, the verb from which these
nouns, *comfort* and *comforter*, are derived often means in classical
and New Testament Greek exactly what the word means in
modern English — to sympathise with and cheer one who is in
grief. As good an illustration of this as any in the New Testament
is 2 *Corinthians* 1: 3-11. But constantly it means much more than
this — and, of course, in the English of earlier centuries the meaning
was much stronger than it is today. Derived from the Latin, con-
fort-ari, the emphasis was upon strengthening (as in *fortify*,
fortification, etc.). So in St. John's Gospel our Lord promises to
send One who would do for the disciples what He Himself had
done, One who would strengthen them and stand by them in times
of weakness. And in 1 *John* 2: 1, Jesus Christ is spoken of, under a
legal simile, as One Who will strengthen the case of a man who
finds himself in the position of being a sinner.

But there is more to the word even than this. There are occurrences of this verb, or of the nouns derived from it, which are not
adequately met either by the idea of comfort in sorrow or strength
in weakness. There is sometimes a hint of what in English is
perhaps best suggested by the noun *stimulation*. The Bayeux

tapestry depicts Bishop Odo at the end of a line of soldiers, belabouring the last man in the line with a club. The legend underneath the picture runs: 'Bishop Odo *comforteth* his soldiers'! The modern equivalent would be *incites, stimulates.*

This, surely, is something of the meaning of the word as it is used in *Romans* 15: 4, with reference to the Old Testament Scriptures. They were written to incite their readers to follow the example of the men of God of old days, to stimulate them so that they might have hope for the future. So, in this prayer, God is described as 'the source of all . . . encouragement', the God who incites the lethargic, who stimulates to brotherly love those who were beginning to live selfishly.

For this is the context of the prayer. The strong are exhorted not to consider themselves, but to accept as their own the tender scruples of the weak, as Christ pleased not Himself. So they were 'to agree with one another after the manner of Christ Jesus' (v. 5, N.E.B.), and the result would be the 'glorifying' of the God and Father of our Lord Jesus Christ. This unanimity of mind 'according to Christ Jesus' — the phrase is very similar to that in *Philippians* 2: 5 ('Let this mind be in you which was also in Christ Jesus') — issues in adoration, glorifying the God and Father of our Lord Jesus Christ. So the Christian, inspired and stimulated by God, reaches his destiny in the worship of God.

Romans 15: 13

A.V.

13. Now the God of hope fill you with all joy and peace in believing, that ye may abound in hope, through the power of the Holy Ghost.

N.E.B.

And may the God of hope fill you with all joy and peace by your faith in him, until, by the power of the Holy Spirit, you overflow with hope.

'The God of hope.' This is the only occurrence in the New Testament of this description of God. It provides us with another instance of a 'mystical genitive', such as we had in v.5. The New English Bible does not help us here, as it did there. Perhaps here, as there, the phrase means that God is the *source* of hope — from Him we derive our hope. Perhaps it means that He is *characterised by* hope; He never despairs; being Himself Love, He 'never faileth' (1 *Corinthians* 13: 8); He never gives us up as hopeless, whereas any human would have despaired of us long ago. Perhaps it means both. I think it does; but of the two streams of meaning in the phrase I suspect the first is the more powerful.

'Faith, hope, and love.' Of the trio, hope has been the neglected member in Christian thought. And not only neglected – it has been misunderstood. 'Hope' in English is often a weak and flabby word. 'I hope it will be fine tomorrow' – what a hope! It will just as likely be wet! The noun must be buttressed by some strong adjectives if it is to say what it is meant to say – 'in *sure and certain* hope of the resurrection'. But in New Testament usage it is a very close cousin to *faith*. Indeed in this prayer, God is described as the God of hope because the word has been suggested by the quotation from *Isaiah* 11: 10 which occupies the previous verse – 'on Him the Gentiles shall set their *hope*' (N.E.B.), pin their expectation, fasten their faith. So in the prayer, it is '*in believing*' ('by your faith in Him', N.E.B.) that the Romans are to be filled with all joy and peace. For a Christian's faith and hope are directed to the living God, to the God who is utterly reliable and whose purposes, however long their fulfilment may tarry, can never finally be frustrated.

This hope is not something which can be worked up by self-effort or which is dependent on a person's psychological make-up. Faith and hope, like prayer itself, are an operation of the Holy Spirit, as also are joy and peace.

We shall see that for St. Paul the word 'hope' has a specific content. It is that the image of God, in which man was created and which has been marred through sin, will be restored (*Ephesians* 1: 18; see pp. 130 ff.). It is this hope, based on the resurrection of Jesus, which robs death of its sting. So William Barclay can comment that for St. Paul 'death is not the abyss of nothingness and annihilation. It is "the gate on the skyline".' He goes on to quote Rupert Brooke:

> 'Safe shall be my going,
> Secretly armed against all death's endeavour;
> Safe though all safety's lost; safe where men fall;
> And if these poor limbs die, safest of all.'
>
> (*More New Testament Words*, pp. 42-3)

Romans 15: 33

A.V.	N.E.B.
33. Now the God of peace be with you all. Amen.	The God of peace be with you all. Amen.

On the meaning of 'peace', see *Romans* 1: 7 (pp. 95 ff.). The phrase 'the God of peace' is a favourite one in the Pauline writings. The apostle promises the Romans that 'the God of peace shall bruise Satan' under their feet (16: 20); he promises the Corinthians that if they live in peace, 'the God of love and peace' will be with them (2 *Corinthians* 13: 11); he makes a similar promise to the Philippians (4: 9); he prays that 'the very God of peace may sanctify' the Thessalonians (1 *Thessalonians* 5: 23) and 'the Lord of peace give them peace' (2 *Thessalonians* 3: 16). Similarly, the author of the Epistle to the Hebrews prays that 'the God of peace . . . may make perfect' his readers (13: 20-21). It is a fine galaxy of passages.

If we ask precisely what the phrase means, we are most likely to find the answer if we translate it as 'the God who is the *source* of peace'. It is He who through the cross and resurrection of Christ has abolished that enmity which must exist where sin casts up a barrier between man and God. This barrier He has annulled. He has created peace. When a man is justified on the basis of faith, he has peace with God through our Lord Jesus Christ (5: 1). A new relationship is established between him and God; the blessings of salvation are his.

It is a great note on which to end the main part of the Epistle, before turning to the greetings which occupy the major part of chapter 16.

Romans 16: 20

A.V.	N.E.B.
20. The grace of our Lord Jesus Christ be with you. Amen.	The grace of our Lord Jesus be with you!

See 2 *Corinthians* 13 : 14 (pp. 117 ff.)

Note—It is only in inferior manuscripts that 'the grace' occurs after verse 23.

Romans 16: 25-27

A.V.	N.E.B.
25. Now to him that is of power to stablish you according to my gospel, and the preaching of Jesus Christ, according to the revelation of the mystery, which was kept secret since the world began,	To him who has power to make your standing sure, according to the Gospel I brought you and the proclamation of Jesus Christ, according to the revelation of that divine secret kept in silence for long ages

A.V.	N.E.B.
26. But now is made manifest, and by the scriptures of the prophets, according to the commandment of the everlasting God, made known to all nations for the obedience of faith :	But now disclosed, and through prophetic scriptures by eternal God's command made known to all nations, to bring them to faith and obedience —
27. To God only wise, be glory through Jesus Christ for ever. Amen.	To God who alone is wise, through Jesus Christ, be glory for endless ages! Amen.

We have called this (p. 94) the longest of the ascriptions with which certain of the New Testament letters end, 'almost creedal in form and in a sense . . . recapitulatory of the main message of the Epistle'. (The shortest form of ascription, if it can be called an ascription at all – it is little more than an ejaculation of worship elicited by a mention of the Deity – is found in the words 'who is blessed for ever, (Amen)'. The occurrences are *Romans* 1: 25; 9: 5; 2 *Corinthians* 11: 31.)

This long ascription is found in some manuscripts here, in others at the end of chapter 14, in others in both places. C. H. Dodd suggests that 'when the last two chapters were removed to make the epistle more suitable for general reading in church, the shortened edition was supplied with a solemn ending in the form of a doxology . . .' (*The Epistle to the Romans*, p. 245, Moffatt Commentary).

The God to whom glory is ascribed is twice described, once in the opening words ('Him who has power to make your standing sure') and once in the closing words ('God who alone is wise'). The rest is parenthesis, though a parenthesis of great weight. The power and the wisdom of God are the basis of the Apostle's doxological outburst. He does not here touch on the power and wisdom of God as seen in Nature – that is a theme on which the Psalmists delighted to ponder (e.g. *Psalms* 19, 104, etc.), and St. Paul touches on it in *Romans* 1: 19 ff. (The reason for the paucity of his references to Nature in this connection can only be guessed at. Was it due to a defect in his make-up? Was it due to a fear of being misunderstood, especially by Gentiles, of a pantheistic approach? Or was it due to the fact that God had manifested Himself to him so overwhelmingly in Christ that His other Self-manifestations were completely outshone? I suspect this had a good deal to do with it.) Here the basis for his praise is God's revelation of Himself in His mighty acts centred in Christ and made known to all nations to bring them to faith and obedience.

The verses touch on most of the main themes of the Epistle which has preceded them — the Gospel so long kept secret but now disclosed, the proclamation of that Gospel, the background of that Gospel in holy Scripture, the destination of that Gospel for all nations, the offering of that Gospel in faith and obedience; and now the power of God in stabilising and strengthening the members of the Church at Rome in the faith of Christ, and the wisdom of God as disclosed in Christ who is Himself wisdom and righteousness and sanctification and redemption (1 *Corinthians* 1: 30).

R. H. Strachan was right in saying of St. Paul: 'His dogmas are all doxologies'.

THE EPISTLES TO THE CORINTHIANS

1 Corinthians 1: 3-9

A.V.	N.E.B.
3. Grace be unto you, and peace, from God our Father, and from the Lord Jesus Christ.	Grace and peace to you from God our Father and the Lord Jesus Christ.
4. I thank my God always on your behalf, for the grace of God which is given you by Jesus Christ;	I am always thanking God for you. I thank him for his grace given to you in Christ Jesus.
5. That in every thing ye are enriched by him, in all utterance, and in all knowledge;	I thank him for all the enrichment that has come to you in Christ. You possess full knowledge and you can give full expression to it,
6. Even as the testimony of Christ was confirmed in you:	Because in you the evidence for the truth of Christ has found confirmation.
7. So that ye come behind in no gift; waiting for the coming of our Lord Jesus Christ:	There is indeed no single gift you lack, while you wait expectantly for our Lord Jesus Christ to reveal himself.
8. Who shall also confirm you unto the end, that ye may be blameless in the day of our Lord Jesus Christ.	He will keep you firm to the end, without reproach on the Day of our Lord Jesus.
9. God is faithful, by whom ye were called unto the fellowship of his Son Jesus Christ our Lord.	It is God himself who called you to share in the life of his Son Jesus Christ our Lord; and God keeps faith.

THE prayer of v. 3 is identical with that in *Romans* 1: 7 (pp. 95 ff.).

Verses 4-9 begin as a thanksgiving and emerge into an expression of confidence in Christ who will keep the Corinthian Christians 'firm to the end' (v. 8) and in the God who keeps faith with those whom He has called (v. 9). So thanksgiving, recollection, and confidence are all interwoven.

On the *grace* of God given us in Christ Jesus, see especially 2 *Corinthians* 13: 14 (pp. 117 ff.). This grace is the ground of their enrichment that has come to them in Christ. St. Paul delights to meditate on the wealth that is theirs in Christ, a wealth made available to them by the voluntary self-impoverishment of Jesus (2 *Corinthians* 8: 9). True, their earthly lot might be a poor one — the Apostle himself had 'suffered the loss of all things'. But 'poor ourselves, we bring wealth to many; penniless, we own the world' (2 *Corinthians* 6: 10, N.E.B.). To know Christ and be found in Him, to be heirs of eternal life — this is wealth, indeed.

The evidence of this wealth is available for all to see. It can be seen in the knowledge and in the ability to express it which is theirs. As a result, men looking at them find in them a witness, a demonstration of the truth which Christ has revealed and which He Himself is (vv. 5-6). And evidence of this wealth can also be seen in those specifically Christian graces, those marks of Christian character (v. 7), which St. Paul elsewhere describes as the harvest of the Spirit (*Galatians* 5: 22-23).

But the Christian is a citizen of two ages. He has received grace as a result of which his wealth is assured and his character deepened. But he also lives in expectation of that future age when Jesus Christ shall come, the Day when He shall be revealed in His full glory (vv. 7b-8). This forward look, this eschatological hope, constituted for the Christians of the first century a strong ethical incentive. 'Everyone who has this hope before him purifies himself, as Christ is pure', St. John was to write only a few decades later (1 *St. John* 3: 3, N.E.B.). We are only at the beginning of the exploration of the wealth that is ours in Christ. More knowledge awaits us, more development of gifts and character — until the Day dawns.

Meanwhile, our confidence is in a God who is utterly reliable, a God who keeps faith, a God who never goes back on His word. This God has called us into the fellowship of His Son, a fellowship which transcends the ages.

On *fellowship*, see 2 *Corinthians* 13: 14; and pp. 120 ff.

1 Corinthians 16: 22

A.V.	N.E.B.
22. Maran-atha.	*Marana tha*–Come, O Lord!

This little prayer has caused much perplexity to the reader of the
Authorised Version, partly because that version has put no punctuation mark after 'anathema' (and made it even more difficult by
spelling it with a capital! It simply means 'accursed' or 'outcast');
partly because it has left the Aramaic words *maran-atha* untrans-
lated; and partly because (in all probability) it has wrongly divided
those words. A full-stop should follow *anathema* — 'if any one does
not love the Lord, let him be outcast'. Then the Apostle looks up
to the Lord. The translation begins 'our Lord' and it is likely that
the verb is in the imperative — *marana tha*, 'O our Lord, come!'
(The retention of Aramaic words in an Epistle written in Greek is
an interesting example of that legacy of Aramaic words which
worship rendered current among Greek-speaking Christians.
Other examples are *abba, alleluia, amen.*)

There has been considerable debate as to what precisely the
Aramaic words mean. It is clear that they have to do with 'the
Lord' or 'our Lord' and with 'coming'. Possibly they mean 'the
Lord (or our Lord) has come' or 'is coming'. If so, they may be
compared to a passage in the Epistle to the Philippians (4: 5-7)
where the fact of the nearness of the Lord leads the Apostle to
remind his readers that they need 'have no anxiety'; their requests
are to be made known to God, and the peace of God will keep
guard over their hearts and their thoughts in Christ Jesus. The
Lord is near — the Lord has come; all is well.

But it is more likely that the words mean, as we have taken them
above to mean, 'O our Lord, come!' In this case, the prayer is
occasioned by the thought of the preceding sentence — there are
those to whom the Lord means little or nothing; the Epistle has
had to deal with such in more instances than one. Then — 'come,
Lord, put the situation right. Come, Lord, bring Thy kingdom in
its fulness. Come, Lord, and reign.' The prayer is similar to that
with which the last book of the New Testament ends, and so is its
setting (*Revelation* 22: 20; see pp. 184 ff.).

The words were used in the early Christian liturgy of the Lord's
Supper. According to *The Didache* (10: 6), the eucharistic thanksgiving ended thus: 'Hosanna to the God of David. If any man is
holy, let him come; if any man is not, let him repent. Maran Atha.
Amen.' Every celebration of the Eucharist was a foretaste of the
heavenly Banquet, and this prayer helped them, week by week, in
looking forward to it.

1 Corinthians 16: 23

A.V.	N.E.B.
23. The grace of our Lord Jesus Christ be with you.	The grace of the Lord Jesus Christ be with you.

See 2 *Corinthians* 13: 14 (pp. 117 ff.)

2 Corinthians 1: 2-4

A.V.	N.E.B.
2. Grace be to you and peace from God our Father, and from the Lord Jesus Christ.	Grace and peace to you from God our Father and the Lord Jesus Christ.
3. Blessed be God, even the Father of our Lord Jesus Christ, the Father of mercies, and the God of all comfort;	Praise be to the God and Father of our Lord Jesus Christ, the all-merciful Father, the God whose consolation never fails us!
4. Who comforteth us in all our tribulation, that we may be able to comfort them which are in any trouble, by the comfort wherewith we ourselves are comforted of God.	He comforts us in all our troubles, so that we in turn may be able to comfort others in any trouble of theirs and to share with them the consolation we ourselves receive from God.

The prayers in the Second Epistle to the Corinthians are brief. Sometimes they are little more than exclamations of gratitude (as, for example, in 2: 14 and 9: 15); sometimes they are yearnings for the Corinthian converts, expressed Godward (as, for example, in 13: 7 ff.). But short though they are, they deserve examination. We are not regarding 9: 10 as a prayer. The Authorised Version does. The Revised Version and the New English Bible are surely right in taking the verbs, which are in the future tense, as straightforward statements of fact.

The prayer of v. 2 is identical with that in *Romans* 1: 7 (pp. 95 ff.).

It is impossible to say where precisely the prayer of thanksgiving, which begins at v. 3, ends. To limit it at v. 4, as we have done, is to be somewhat arbitrary; but it will serve our purpose. The truth is that what begins as a thanksgiving ends in a meditation which itself issues in a bit of personal history. The apostle is thinking Godwards.

God is here described as 'the Father of our Lord Jesus Christ.'

Professor John Burnaby points out that, in the New Testament
Epistles, there is an absence of all express teaching about God as
Father of *men*. Further, the Father-name is almost exclusively
appropriated to formulae of salutation, blessing, and confession —
in all of which it is constantly linked with the name of Jesus Christ.
'Thus for St. Paul Fatherhood and Sonship are strictly Christological terms: the divine fatherhood is by no means a commonplace
— it has been *revealed* in Christ. *It is as the Father of Jesus Christ
that God has made himself known*' (*The Belief of Christendom*, p. 23).

The dominant theme of the passage is that of comfort. God, the
all-merciful Father, is described as 'the God of all comfort'. If it be
thought that to emphasise this strand of Christian truth is to run
the danger of emphasising the 'soft' side of the Christian faith, St.
Paul at once maintains that God's comfort is given us *so that* we in
turn may be able to comfort others in trouble.

It is no use to blind ourselves to the fact that the world is so
constituted that a great many people get hurt. Men and women are
so made that, often because of their own folly, they get hurt. All of
us, because of our egocentricity, hurt others and, for that matter,
ourselves. It is all very well to say: 'Better to erect a fence at the
top of the precipice than to provide an ambulance at the bottom'.
Of course. The Church at its best has sought to do just this. But
ambulance work, healing work, consolatory work has always been a
big part of the Church's ministry — and will be, so long as men sin
and wound and hurt one another.

The ministry of Jesus was a ministry of healing and of comfort.
He could — He did — denounce the proud and the self-satisfied. He
condemned those who laid a heavy burden of religious scrupulosity
on others and did not lift a finger to help them. But, through and
through, from beginning to end, the ministry of Jesus was concerned with comfort. Not indeed, let it be said, the superficial kind
of comfort which men sometimes minister; but the comfort which,
having probed the wound deeply, can really heal it. Thus at the
start of His public ministry, Jesus made His own the programme of
the prophet which included the words: 'He hath sent me to bind
up the broken-hearted ... to comfort all that mourn ...' (*Isaiah* 61:
1-2). He said to the woman who was a sinner: 'Thy faith hath saved
thee; go in peace' (*St. Luke* 7: 50). Like the God whose servant He
was, He healed the diseases (*Psalms* 103: 3), physical, mental,
and spiritual, of the people. He was the Representative of the God
of whom it was said, with infinite tenderness, that He would 'wipe
away tears from off all faces' (*Isaiah* 25: 8; cp. *Revelation* 21: 4).

Such was the ministry of Jesus. Such is the ministry of His Church, the company of the comforted who themselves are able to share with the needy 'the consolation we ourselves receive from God' (v. 4, N.E.B.).

2 Corinthians 2: 14

A.V.	N.E.B.
14. Now thanks be unto God, which always causeth us to triumph in Christ, and maketh manifest the savour of his knowledge by us in every place.	But thanks be to God, who continually leads us about, captives in Christ's triumphal procession, and everywhere uses us to reveal and spread abroad the fragrance of the knowledge of himself!

Here is an exclamation of gratitude, uttered against a background of perplexity and pain. (The opening verses of the chapter should be read carefully if the Apostle's position is to be understood.) But in it and through it all, he can exclaim: 'Thanks be to God!'

He illustrates the truth he is trying to expound by using the analogy of an imperial Roman triumph. The commander, who has been away from the capital on some military expedition, returns, bringing his captives with him. They grace his triumph, as the conquering hero marches through the city – sights, sounds, and smells of incense all combining to make the occasion unforgettable.

That is the general picture given in this prayer of thanksgiving. The precise and detailed meaning is not altogether clear. It may be that St. Paul means, as the Authorised Version indicates, that God causes us to triumph in Christ. It is more probable that he means that God leads us in triumph (with Him) in Christ – so the Revised Version. Or it may mean that God 'leads us about, captives in Christ's triumphal procession' – so the New English Bible. Captives indeed we are, but thankful to be so, for in that captivity we have found our freedom –

> 'Imprison me within Thine arms,
> And strong shall be my hand'.
> (G. Matheson)

The second half of the verse pursues the picture further. The procession sweeps on. The incense rises. It is the incense of the knowledge of God and His Gospel which is shed abroad through the apostolic agency. True, it smells differently in different nostrils, depending on the kind of person to whom the scent of the 'incense' comes. The apostolic ministry is a mysterious ministry, for it is a ministry of that word of God which is 'sharper than any two-edged sword'. To some – to those on the way to life – it savours of life. To others – to those on the way to perdition – it savours of death (vv. 15-16).

The issues of such a ministry are so momentous as to make the calling heavy with responsibility – 'who is equal to such a calling?' (v. 16, N.E.B.). But weighty though the responsibility is, to be entrusted with such a ministry is cause for deepest thanksgiving to God. Hence the gratitude of this prayer.

2 Corinthians 9: 15

A.V.	N.E.B.
15. Thanks be unto God for his unspeakable gift.	Thanks be to God for his gift beyond words!

God's 'unspeakable gift', His 'gift beyond words', is Jesus Christ. Of that there can be no doubt. But this exclamatory prayer of gratitude comes at the end of a long passage, comprising chapters 8 and 9, on Church finance. Is there any connection between the two? Indeed there is! Christian giving can only be *Christian* giving when it is done out of sheer gratitude for The Gift. If that could be grasped and acted upon, we should be well on the way to finding the solution to the financial problems by which, all too often, we are harassed.

These two remarkable chapters lay down most of the essential principles of Christian giving. We may briefly glance at them. The members of the congregations in Macedonia in the first instance offered *themselves* to the Lord (8: 5). Until that is done, giving is a burden, a matter of 'nicely calculated less or more' – how much *must* I give? But once a man has seen the generosity of our Lord Jesus Christ, His self-giving for our enrichment (8: 9), and has given back to Him the life he owes, the whole atmosphere is changed. An eager desire to give (8: 12, N.E.B.) seizes him. He thinks the matter out, decides responsibly, and gives cheerfully (9: 7), working on the principle 'sparse sowing, sparse reaping; bountiful sowing, bountiful reaping'. There is no grudging – it is 'a piece of willing service' (9: 12) as well as an act of down-to-earth obedience to God (9: 13).

Christian giving is *thanksgiving*, a systematic act of gratitude to the God who so loved the world that He gave it His gift beyond words.

2 Corinthians 13: 7-10

A.V.	N.E.B.
7. Now I pray to God that ye do no evil; not that we should appear approved, but that ye should do that which is honest, though we be as reprobates.	Our prayer to God is that we may not have to hurt you; we are not concerned to be vindicated ourselves; we want you to do what is right, even if we should seem to be discredited.
8. For we can do nothing against the truth, but for the truth.	For we have no power to act against the truth, but only for it.
9. For we are glad, when we are weak, and ye are strong: and this also we wish, even your perfection.	We are well content to be weak at any time if only you are strong. Indeed, my whole prayer is that all may be put right with you.
10. Therefore I write these things being absent, lest being present I should use sharpness, according to the power which the Lord hath given me to edification, and not to destruction.	My purpose in writing this letter before I come, is to spare myself, when I come, any sharp exercise of authority—authority which the Lord gave me for building up and not for pulling down.

This is the prayer of a pastor for his people. He looks up to God on their behalf—twice he uses the verb 'to pray' (vv. 7, 9). He looks out upon them in their need. His past dealings with them have not all been easy. There have been matters for which he has been in duty bound sternly to rebuke them. There has been that grave letter which he has had to send them. He has had to hurt them, as a surgeon has to hurt before he can heal. Now he prays that he will not have to do it again (v. 7, N.E.B.)—he cares not about himself or his reputation.

The nub of the prayer comes at the end of v. 9. The New English Bible translates 'my whole prayer is that all may be put right with you'—with perhaps a hint of the righting of personal relationships between Apostle and Corinthians. That may be a correct interpretation. The original is essentially simple—'and this I pray, your perfecting' (A.V. 'perfection'; R.V. 'perfecting'). The idea behind that word is that of mending what is broken; it can be used of nets, or bones, or character. What is in St. Paul's mind at this point? Their mutual relationship? Their by no means perfected Christian character? Which? Both, perhaps. We cannot tell. The very ambiguity affords us material for use in prayer.

2 Corinthians 13: 14

A.V.	N.E.B.
14. The grace of the Lord Jesus Christ, and the love of God, and the communion of the Holy Ghost, be with you all. Amen.	The grace of the Lord Jesus Christ, and the love of God, and fellowship in the Holy Spirit, be with you all.

This is the only occurrence in the New Testament of the full 'Trinitarian' form of the prayer which we describe as 'the Grace' (p. 94). It calls for fairly careful examination.

We may note that the order of the clauses reflects very often the order of Christian experience. Times without number in the story of men's search for reality, beginning with the historic fact of Jesus Christ, the 'grace' of His Person and work, men have been led on to dare to believe in the love of God and in that fellowship of the Holy Spirit which finds its chief expression in the Church of God. God moves men, and brings them to Himself, in an infinite variety of ways. There is no set order or stereotyped pattern. But very often it proves to be the case that Christ's grace is the door-way, the entrance-gate, to a man's realisation of God's love and the Spirit's fellowship.

'The *grace* of our Lord Jesus Christ.' The word is a delightful one, used in classical literature of beauty of form. St. Luke uses it of the first sermon that Jesus preached in His home town of Nazareth – 'they were surprised that words of such grace should fall from His lips' (4: 22, N.E.B.). They were winsome words. The sheer attractiveness of His message won a hearing and held people's attention; it drew a sigh of surprise that religion could be such a lovely thing as Jesus made it that day.

But *grace* has a deeper religious and theological significance in the New Testament. It indicates the outgoing, forgiving activity of God, totally undeserved, to men and women who have gone wrong.

It is at this point that the teachings of our Lord and of St. Paul meet – that the latter can be seen to be a faithful interpretation of the former. Take, for example, the parable of Jesus (*St. Luke*

7: 41 ff.) in which He tells the story of the two debtors, one owing a paltry sum, the other an enormous sum, but both at one in their complete inability to pay. At the point of their deep need, when they had nothing to offer, the man to whom the money was owed 'graced' them both. The verb is that from which the noun *grace* is derived — 'he graced them, he forgave them both'. They could face life again with the burden gone.

Or again, the parable of the Prodigal Son (*St. Luke* 15: 11 ff.) is another illustration of the same point. The father 'graced' the younger boy, when he had nothing but his rags to offer. He would have 'graced' the older boy, too, if he had been given half a chance — only the supercilious pride of the respectable son stood in the way as an impregnable barrier to the reception of that grace.

The teaching of Jesus is full of this; He spent His ministry in giving Himself away to sinners. He was much more comfortable in their company than He was in the respectable company of the proud. And at the end, having given Himself away to sinners all His life, He emptied Himself for sinners on the cross.

'Ye know the grace of our Lord Jesus Christ, that, though He was rich, yet for your sakes He became poor, that ye through His poverty might be rich' (2 *Corinthians* 8: 9). There is the theme regnant of the ministry of Jesus. And there is the theme regnant of the Epistles of St. Paul — 'God commendeth His love toward us, in that, while we were yet sinners, Christ died for us' (*Romans* 5: 8). 'Forgiving one another, even as God for Christ's sake "graced" you' (*Ephesians* 4: 32).

This theme of the reinstatement of men and women who have gone wrong is the powerful, cathartic, central theme of the Christian faith. No wonder that this prayer, which has so gripped the Christian imagination as to come next in popular use to the Lord's Prayer, should begin with 'the grace of our Lord Jesus Christ'.

'And the *love* of God.' How can one talk about — still more, how can one believe in — the love of God in view of the suffering by which creation is marred? Here is the glaring incongruity by which every thinking man is faced — a world so utterly beautiful, but its creatures, at all levels, marked and marred by evil and by suffering. Life is all too full of examples. One which springs to mind may suffice. I had been tramping in the Swiss Alps, surrounded by indescribable beauty of tree and flower, of water and snow, of hill and dale. One's whole being was satisfied with the vast expanse of natural beauty, and one's mind turned to the God of whom this beauty was but a dim reflection. I sat down for a drink outside a little chalet high in the mountains. Nearby, an old lady was working at her spinning wheel. Dressed in the fashion of the place, she was a picturesque figure. She had a beauty of expression which surely must have betokened an inward beauty of character. But her hands! They were distorted, I had almost said beyond recognition, by rheumatism which must have caused her acute pain for a very long time. One had moved among suffering for many years; but here, somehow, the incongruity of it all smote one. All this beauty around one — and then, *that*?

It is an old problem, and one which has puzzled the wisest of men since first they began to think. The Greeks hammered at it, obsessed particularly with the question: 'Where does evil come from ?' The Hebrews hammered at it, obsessed not so much with the problem of its source as of its analysis and its mastery — this thing is here; how do we battle with it? How overcome it? How win?

What has Christianity to say about it? I do not believe that Christianity claims to give us a complete solution of the problems presented to us by nature and by history — the problems of sin and disease and premature death. We had better face that fact and accept it. But I do believe that Christianity puts within our grasp a torch, sufficiently clear in its light to show the way for us to walk in, step by step, in a life of faith and trust and service and battle. And at the place called Calvary — 'in the garden secretly, and on the cross on high' — we get such light as shines from no other place. 'God loved like that' — so says the cross; and the God of inexorable order is seen to be also the God of infinite grace.

Professor James S. Stewart, in the last chapter of his book *The Strong Name*, wrestles with this matter of the love of God. 'Is it true?' he asks. 'Is love sovereign? Is God upon the throne?' In reply, he writes:

'I want you to realise that the only way to answer that question decisively is the way by which Paul reached his answer. You can never be absolutely sure that righteous love is on the throne of the universe, until you have met redeeming grace in the secret place of your own soul. Or rather, let me turn that round now, and say — you cannot experience the grace of Jesus, and ever doubt the love of God again. If once at the cross you have seen Christ facing the full force of life's tragic mystery, all the concentrated might of suffering, sin, and death, and conquering in His love, then you know that here is a power which has come forth from the very heart of reality, from the bosom of the Father, and shall yet subdue all things unto itself. "The grace of the Lord Jesus Christ, and"—through that—"the love of God" ' (pp. 257 and 258).

The life and thought of Albert Schweitzer are very interesting in this connection. He saw the problem of evil as frankly insoluble. From the viewpoint of the *spectator*, he found it impossible to extract any intelligible meaning from life—there was a radical evil at the heart of things, baffling and defeating. But, leaving behind him a scintillating career in Europe where he had distinguished himself in philosophy and theology, in music and in medicine, he went off to Lambarene, plunging into a veritable maelstrom of disease and darkness, and there he achieved an intensely affirmative attitude to life. He could not fully understand the marring process which brought so incongruous a discord into the beauty of God's world. He continued to probe and explore and think. But he could fight; and in fighting and in partially overcoming, his life found fulfilment.

It was the way the Master went. Jesus plunged in, emptying Himself in the process. Jesus believed in the love of God, taught that love, demonstrated that love and, in a profound sense, *was* the love of God in action. If that is so, we can hold on, and dare to believe—and to fight.

'And the *communion* of the Holy Spirit'. If we are to understand the meaning of communion, of fellowship, we had best begin with the earthly ministry of Jesus. It was one of His greatest achievements that He created a fellowship out of that strange group of men and women whom He called to Him—the inner group of the Twelve and the larger group of disciples. It was a significant achievement that could draw together a Simon the Zealot, fired with a passion for home rule for Palestine, with a Matthew the tax-gatherer who, because he earned his living from the Roman invader, must have seemed a traitor to Simon. But Jesus called these political opposites, and knit them into a fellowship of loyalty to Him; and in that loyalty they found love for one another. So again, He called John, young, sensitive, mystical in outlook, and knit him into a fellowship with Peter, rough, outspoken, impetuous. In common loyalty to Him, they found themselves in fellowship with one another. And Mary Magdalene 'from whom He had cast out seven devils'—poor soul, was she a woman of the streets as tradition would have it? She was drawn into the circle, together with Joanna who moved in court circles — so St. Luke tells us (8: 2-3).

Political barriers, personal barriers, social barriers — all fall before the personality of Jesus, and a fellowship is created focused in Him.

But surely the fellowship of people like these, so different in personal characteristics and background, could not possibly continue after the death of the One who was its focus? The miracle happened. It did continue. More — it deepened, and extended its bounds. It made room for a stormy petrel like Saul of Tarsus (though his admission filled some of the members with foreboding (*Acts* 9: 26)). Pentecost saw a swift and sudden extension. Within the fellowship, that fellowship of the Holy Spirit of Jesus, the old barriers which separated one from another with such dreadful efficacy, seemed to avail no more. As St. Paul put it: In Christ 'there can be no such thing as Jew and Greek' (the racial barrier is gone); 'slave and freeman' (the class barrier is gone); 'male and female' (the sex barrier is gone) (*Galatians* 3: 28). Loyalty to Him means that these barriers sink into insignificance. The fellowship of the incarnate Jesus has now become the fellowship of the Holy Spirit, and the withdrawal of His physical presence has made no difference to its continuance; indeed, it has opened up the way to its extension and its deepening.

Now this fellowship, just because it is the fellowship of the Spirit who is the Creator Spirit, is itself a creative thing. Consider its creative nature. The members of the fellowship find that, under the activity of the Spirit, the historic Christ becomes a contemporary Person. Thus, Jesus is not simply one of the ancient Hebrews, not even the greatest of the Hebrew prophets, or the greatest of the world's religious teachers to be listed with the immortals. No; to the Christian believer He becomes, through the Spirit, a contemporary, closer to him than breathing, nearer than hands and feet.

So, within this fellowship of the Spirit, the Creator Spirit creates out of the dead text of Scripture a living word. Within the Church, views of the meaning of the inspiration of Scripture differ widely. But there would be general agreement on the fact that, in every age,

> 'The Spirit breathes upon the word,
> And brings the truth to light'.

To the thinking and obedient disciple, the word of Jesus comes alive, 'living and powerful'. For the Spirit is the 'One through whom time and distance are annihilated, and through whom the word of Jesus becomes the living and contemporary word . . .' (Stephen Neill, *The Interpretation of the New Testament, 1861-1961*, p. 235).

Again, within this fellowship of the Spirit, He creates, out of the rough stuff of unholy men, saints of God. St. Augustine was no model of morality as a youth, but the Holy Spirit made him one of the saints. So with a Luther, a Wesley, a Carlile, a Pope John XXIII. Yes – and so with the unknown saints, many of them unlettered, men whose sheer holiness silences the brashness of those who confuse knowledge with the wisdom of the Lord.

So the Holy Spirit creates – recreates – in every age the Body of Christ, where differences are not merely annihilated but transcended, creatively incorporated into the fulness of the Body. The fellowship of the Holy Spirit is a very exciting thing.

THE EPISTLE TO THE GALATIANS

Galatians 1: 3-5

A.V.	N.E.B.
3. Grace be to you and peace from God the Father, and from our Lord Jesus Christ,	Grace and peace to you from God the Father and our Lord Jesus Christ,
4. Who gave himself for our sins, that he might deliver us from this present evil world, according to the will of God and our Father:	Who sacrificed himself for our sins, to rescue us out of this present age of wickedness, as our God and Father willed:
5. To whom be glory for ever and ever. Amen.	To whom be glory for ever and ever. Amen.

THE opening verse is identical with *Romans* 1: 7 (pp. 95 ff.). Mention of our Lord Jesus Christ strikes a note which makes the Apostle postpone the main message of his letter, the rebuke which begins at v. 6. It is as if the frown must wait until he has had time for a brief eulogy of Jesus. This occupies vv. 4-5.

It is instructive to notice what he fastens on as the ground of his doxology ('to whom be glory for ever and ever. Amen'). It is not the teaching of Jesus, nor the fact that He 'went about doing good', nor His example which we should follow. These are great things, all of them causes for deep thanksgiving. But here he by-passes them, to fasten on Christ's sacrifice for our sins and on His rescue of us. He looks straight at the cross, where man's deepest problem, his sins, was radically dealt with. He puts his finger firmly on Christ's death as the deed by which deliverance came to men. 'God forbid', he was to write later in this same letter, 'that I should glory, save in the cross of our Lord Jesus Christ' (6: 14).

The purpose of Christ's redeeming work is stated to be 'that He might deliver us from this present evil world'. St. Paul touches lightly on the familiar idea of the two ages, the present age characterised by the powerful presence of sin and evil, and the coming age in which God's sovereignty will be fully asserted and His kingdom brook no rival. That was good Jewish doctrine, and the language here used is redolent of it. But there is a difference, and this difference pinpoints the distinctive contribution that the work of Jesus has made. Deliverance from this present evil age is for the Christian not merely a hope for the future – it is that, in its fulness. It is also a fact of the present. Already, while living *in* the world, he is delivered *from* it. To put it in Johannine terminology, eternal life belongs to the here and now, though its consummation is awaited. 'He that believeth on the Son hath everlasting life' (*St. John* 3: 36). Already the believer is a citizen of both worlds, an heir of both ages. He is 'delivered', while he awaits the final deliverance (*Romans* 8: 15, 23). Here is the tension which gives meaning to his life and power to his witness (see pp. 68 ff.).

Galatians 6: 16

A.V.	N.E.B.
16. And as many as walk according to this rule, peace be on them, and mercy, and upon the Israel of God.	Whoever they are who take this principle for their guide, peace and mercy be upon them, and upon the whole Israel of God!

This is half a goodwill wish and half a prayer. Professor G. S. Duncan calls it 'a prayer for peace' (*The Epistle to the Galatians*, p. 192, Moffatt Commentary), so we may consider it briefly here.

On *peace*, see pp. 95 ff.

On *mercy*, see p. 160.

The 'rule' (A.V.; 'principle', N.E.B.) to which St. Paul here refers is the principle of 'new creation' which he has just mentioned (v. 15). Ezekiel had spoken of the 'new spirit', the 'heart of flesh', that God would give to His people (11: 19). St. Paul elsewhere speaks of the 'new creation' which takes place when a man comes to be 'in Christ' (2 *Corinthians* 5: 17). 'The only thing that counts is new creation!' (v. 15, N.E.B.). External things such as circumcision are irrelevant. The particular race to which a man belongs by natural birth is irrelevant. All that matters is that he should belong to that 'third race' which incorporates both Jews and Gentiles, the 'Israel of God'. To be 'very members incorporate' in that race, 'in the mystical body' of the Son of God, 'the blessed company of all faithful (believing) people', this is true blessedness; this is to experience the peace and mercy of God.

The theme is elaborated in *Ephesians* 3 (see pp. 133 ff.).

Galatians 6: 18

A.V.   N.E.B.

18. Brethren, the grace of our Lord Jesus Christ be with your spirit. Amen.	The grace of our Lord Jesus Christ be with your spirit, my brothers. Amen.

The ending is similar to that with which many of the Epistles close (p. 94). But there is an addition. It is the simple words 'my brothers'. They occur in no other ending. It is a touch the significance of which should not be missed.

Of all the Pauline Epistles, that to the Galatians is the most severe. In it, the Apostle 'thunders and lightens and speaks sheer flame' (Erasmus). They were senseless; they were bewitched; they were quickly turning away from the One who called them; they were following a different gospel which was not a gospel at all. Phrase is piled on excoriating phrase to denounce their folly, their apostasy. And as for those who, by insisting on circumcision, upset the faith of the Galatian believers, 'they had better go the whole way and make eunuchs of themselves!' (5: 12, N.E.B.). There are, indeed, tender touches – the Apostle is a mother 'travailing in birth' for her children (4: 19). His pastoral care shines through the fierceness of his rebukes. But over all, the tone of the Epistle is severe.

How shall he end it? He will use the familiar words of the Grace, with all its undertones of graciousness and forgiveness. And he will add 'my brothers'. They are that, for all their folly and waywardness – his brothers in Christ.

'Brother' had for him a special significance. When the light had flashed on him on the Damascus road, and Saul the persecutor had become Paul the Apostle, Ananias was sent to him to restore his sight. Little wonder that Ananias had demurred (*Acts* 9: 13; and see pp. 84 ff.). But, swallowing his forebodings, he went and – are not these some of the tenderest words in the New Testament? – he 'laid his hands on him and said, "Saul, *my brother* . . ." ' (*Acts* 9: 17, N.E.B.).

'The grace of our Lord Jesus Christ be with your spirit, *my brothers.*'

THE EPISTLE TO THE
EPHESIANS

Ephesians 1: 2

A.V.

N.E.B.

2. Grace be to you, and peace, from God our Father, and from the Lord Jesus Christ.

Grace to you and peace from God our Father and the Lord Jesus Christ.

The prayer is identical with that in *Romans* 1: 7 (pp. 95 ff.)

Ephesians 1: 15-23

A.V.

N.E.B.

15. Wherefore I also, after I heard of your faith in the Lord Jesus, and love unto all the saints,

Because of all this, now that I have heard of the faith you have in the Lord Jesus and of the love you bear towards all God's people,

16. Cease not to give thanks for you, making mention of you in my prayers;

I never cease to give thanks for you when I mention you in my prayers.

17. That the God of our Lord Jesus Christ, the Father of glory, may give unto you the spirit of wisdom and revelation in the knowledge of him:

I pray that the God of our Lord Jesus Christ, the all-glorious Father, may give you the spiritual powers of wisdom and vision, by which there comes the knowledge of him.

18. The eyes of your understanding being enlightened; that ye may know what is the hope of his calling, and what the riches of the glory of his inheritance in the saints,

I pray that your inward eyes may be illumined, so that you may know what is the hope to which he calls you, what the wealth and glory of the share he offers you among his people in their heritage,

19. And what is the exceeding greatness of his power to us-ward who believe, according to the working of his mighty power,

And how vast the resources of his power open to us who trust in him.

A.V.	N.E.B.
20. Which he wrought in Christ, when he raised him from the dead, and set him at his own right hand in the heavenly places,	They are measured by his strength and the might which he exerted in Christ when he raised him from the dead, when he enthroned him at his right hand in the heavenly realms,
21. Far above all principality, and power, and might, and dominion, and every name that is named, not only in this world, but also in that which is to come:	Far above all government and authority, all power and dominion, and any title of sovereignty that can be named, not only in this age but in the age to come.
22. And hath put all things under his feet, and gave him to be the head over all things to the church,	He put everything in subjection beneath his feet, and appointed him as supreme head to the church,
23. Which is his body, the fulness of him that filleth all in all.	Which is his body and as such holds within it the fullness of him who himself receives the entire fullness of God.

THE prayers in the Epistle to the Ephesians (1: 15-23; 3: 14-21) are two of the greatest in the New Testament. We should recall that the letter was most probably an encyclical, sent to a number of churches in Asia Minor of which the Church at Ephesus was one. The words 'at Ephesus' (1: 1) are missing in the best manuscripts, and the letter has no personal greetings or particular allusions. (The reference to Tychicus in 6: 21, is hardly an exception to this.) Here, almost better than anywhere else, we can hear St. Paul praying for what C. S. Lewis calls 'our great, permanent, objective necessities' (*Letters to Malcolm Chiefly on Prayer*, p. 22). There is nothing petty or narrow in these prayers. The horizon is wide; the scope unlimited.

The prayer in chapter 1 issues out of praise; that in chapter 3 out of meditation. We must pause to glance at the hymn of praise (vv. 3-14) which forms the background of this prayer.

This hymn is trinitarian in shape, the refrain 'to the praise of His glory' or 'to the praise of the glory of His grace' referring first to Christ (v. 6), secondly to the Father (v. 12), and thirdly to the Spirit (v. 14). It soars into 'the heavenly realms' (v. 3). It embraces 'the universe, all in heaven and on earth' (v. 10, N.E.B.). It is Christ-centred — we note its healthy objectivity in the frequent recurrence of 'in Christ', 'in the Beloved', and 'in Him' (and contrast the petty subjectivity of some sub-Christian hymnody!). And yet it is a hymn which, if we may so express it, has its feet firmly on the earth. The Apostle's memory goes back to one here, a group there, in the churches which he had founded or built up, who received 'the seal of the Holy Spirit' given in baptism (v. 13). When he thinks of that Spirit, he refers to Him as the 'earnest' or 'pledge' that we shall enter upon our heritage (v. 14). The word 'earnest' is little used today. More is the pity. The poet used it well when he wrote:

> 'The primrose flower peeps forth
> To give an earnest of the spring.'
>
> (Wordsworth)

The word used by the writer of this Epistle is that used in modern Greek for an engagement ring – it is a pledge that he who gives it intends to see the business through! So God, in giving the Spirit, gives a pledge that, in His mercy, He intends to see through to its great conclusion the work that He has begun in us – 'we shall enter upon our heritage'. God, having set His hand to the plough, will not look back.

There, in briefest outline, is the great sweep of the eulogistic hymn out of which our prayer issues like some mountain waterfall issuing from a mighty glacier.

But there are reasons nearer home which give the writer cause for thanksgiving. He has heard news which has made him glad. In these churches in Asia Minor are men and women with a living *faith* in the Lord Jesus and with a *love* which goes out towards all God's people (v. 15). Faith and love – two of the three great gifts which he mentions elsewhere (1 *Corinthians* 13: 13); if they have these graces, all will be well. It is cause for ceaseless thanksgiving. That first – and then prayer. To this we may now turn our attention.

On 'making mention of you in my prayers' see *Romans* 1: 9; and p. 98. St. Paul sees them in his mind's eye, with all their strengths and all their weaknesses. One by one he 'mentions' them, holds them up before God, as one might hold up a sick child to the beneficial rays of the sun.

The prayer is closely packed. Phrase is piled on phrase. It is a torrent that pours. We may best approach it by asking two questions: *First, to whom* does the Apostle pray? *Secondly, what* does he pray?

i. *To whom does he pray?* The answer is (*a*) to 'the God of our Lord Jesus Christ' — a somewhat mysterious phrase (v. 17). What does 'of' mean? It must mean the God to whom Jesus prayed. His God is our God. 'I ascend unto my Father, and your Father; and to my God, and your God' (*St. John* 20: 17). The God to whom He prayed in the intimacy of an unbroken communion is the same God to whom we come, however falteringly and with however dim a vision. But 'the God of our Lord Jesus Christ' means more than this. It means the God whom Jesus disclosed; the God of whom He spoke especially in terms of kingship and fatherhood. In our praying to Him, then, we must never think unworthily; never allow a conception of Him incompatible with the teaching of Jesus to enter our mind. (*b*) He prays, further, to 'the Father of (the) glory' — a phrase unique in the New Testament. The New English Bible paraphrases this as 'the all-glorious Father'. It is just conceivable that 'the glory' may be a reference to Jesus Christ Himself, in which case 'the Father of the Glory' would be equivalent to the first phrase, 'the God of our Lord Jesus Christ'. But it is more likely that the phrase is intended to indicate the majesty of the God to whom those who pray can only come with awe.

ii. *What does he pray?* The answer, at its briefest, is to be found in the second half of v. 17. These brief, tightly packed phrases are elaborated in vv. 18-19. First, then, we look at the essence of the prayer, the prayer in its most concentrated form — that God 'may give you the spiritual powers of wisdom and vision, by which there comes the knowledge of Him' (N.E.B.). More literally, we may translate, 'a spirit of wisdom and unveiling in an experimental knowledge of Him'. *Wisdom* — there is a whole body of Jewish literature which has come to be known as the Wisdom Literature, of which the Books of *Proverbs* and of *Wisdom* are to most English readers the best known (*Wisdom* chs. 8 ff. are especially worthy of study). Here we see an elaboration of the kind of theme set out in, e.g., *Proverbs* 8-9. In such writings as these, Wisdom is hypostatised (semi-personalised). In this way, the doctrine of Wisdom became seminal in the elaboration of the doctrine of the Word, and its influence can be traced in such great Christological passages as *St. John* 1, *Colossians* 1 and *Hebrews* 1. 'O send her out of Thy holy heavens . . . that being present she may labour with me, that I may know what is pleasing unto Thee.' So the old Wisdom writer had written in a prayer somewhat similar to this of St. Paul (*Wisdom* 9: 10).

'*Unveiling*' — the word is explained in v. 18, 'your inward eyes . . .

illumined' (N.E.B.). It signifies the drawing aside of a curtain
which hides. 'Draw from our timid eyes the veil . . .' Most of us go
through life with our eyes half shut, blind to 'the many-splendoured
thing'. The sights and sounds around us combine to cast a veil over
our eyes and so we miss the knowledge of Him.

'*Knowledge.*' This is knowledge with a difference. The usual
Greek word for knowledge is *gnosis*. But here and often elsewhere
St. Paul adds a prefix, making the word *epignosis*. It is as if he
would say, by the very form of the word which he uses: 'Intellectual knowledge *by itself* is not enough. The Greeks tried the way of
the intellect, but to them the cross was only folly. More than
intellect is called for. Knowledge must be brought into the sphere
of spiritual experience'. There is an interesting passage in *The
Journal of a Soul* in which the future Pope John XXIII, then in
preparation for his ordination as a priest, wrote during a retreat:
'God preserve me from underestimating study, but I must beware
of attaching to it an exaggerated and absolute value. Study is one
eye, the left eye; if the right one is missing, what is the use of a
single eye, of study by itself? After all, what am I now that I have
secured my degree? Nothing, a poor ignorant fellow. What use am I
to the Church with that alone? . . . In future I shall study with even
more enthusiasm than before, but I shall call things by their right
names; I shall be studying not so much for the examinations as for
life itself, so that what I learn will become an integral part of me'
(p. 156). It is a good commentary on *gnosis* and *epignosis*, on the
difference between intellectual furniture and knowledge of life —
of Life — 'the knowledge of Him'. 'That I may know Him'
(*Philippians* 3: 10) — this is the experimental knowledge of Christ
which is life indeed. Knowledge by itself all too easily 'breeds
conceit; it is love that builds' (see 1 *Corinthians* 8: 1-3).

Here, then, in the second half of v. 17, is the core of the prayer.
It is elaborated in the next two verses:

'The eyes of your understanding being enlightened' (A.V.);
'your inward eyes . . . illumined' (N.E.B.); 'the eyes of your heart
being enlightened' (Greek) — the heart being the seat of affection
and will, vision must lead to action; illumination to decision.

That prayer being granted, what will follow? Three things:

First, they will know 'what is the hope to which God calls them'.
In the Pauline writings, 'hope' is no vague word. It has a quite
clear and definite connotation. It is the specific hope — confidence —
that the image of God in which man was made, which has been
marred and defaced by sin, will be restored. 'We rejoice in hope of

the glory of God' (*Romans* 5: 2), 'the divine splendour that is to be ours' (N.E.B.). 'Such a hope is no mockery, because God's love has flooded our inmost heart through the Holy Spirit He has given us' (*Romans* 5: 5, N.E.B.). St. John, in a superb passage, echoes this thought (1 *St. John* 3: 2-3): 'this hope' is precisely that 'we shall be like Him; for we shall see Him as He is'. *This* is the hope to which God calls us.

Secondly, they will know what are 'the riches of the glory of His inheritance in the saints'. The New English Bible translation here is a free one – 'what the wealth and glory of the share He offers you among His people in their heritage'. This may be right – it is as much an interpretation as a translation. It is in keeping with the thought of the Epistle, elaborated especially in chapters 2 and 3, that Gentiles share with Jews in the redemption which God has made known in Christ. Those who hitherto were 'far off' now share in the heritage of God's people. But is not another interpretation at least possible, perhaps likely? We may put it thus: *God* has an inheritance. It consists of 'the saints', that is, the Church, 'the blessed company of all faithful people'. In the Old Testament, Israel was referred to as God's 'glory' (e.g. *Psalms* 78: 61 – He 'delivered . . . His *glory* into the enemy's hand'). This is in keeping with that concept. Now St. Paul ponders on God's *wealth* in such an inheritance. The Psalmist (149: 4) had said that 'the Lord taketh pleasure in His people'. Why should not St. Paul exult in the thought of God's wealth in the Church which He had bought at the price of the blood of His Son?

Thirdly, they will know 'how vast' are 'the resources of His power open to us who trust in Him' (N.E.B.). This power, the writer is swift to point out, can only be measured in terms of the power of God supremely manifested in the resurrection of Jesus from the dead. Just as in Old Testament days, the power of God had been signally manifested – the strength of His arm shown – in rescuing His people from tyranny under the Egyptians, so now 'the greatness of His power' is to be seen in the resurrection of Jesus. But the demonstration of that power did not cease on the first Easter Day. We 'who trust in Him' share in that power – share in that resurrection, as one day we shall fully share in His glory.

Here, strictly speaking, the prayer itself may be said to end. It tones off into an elaboration of the point the Apostle has just made about the power of God as seen in Christ's resurrection and ascension-enthronement. The language of v. 21 is probably coloured by the language of those Gnostic sects who thought of a

kind of ladder of intermediary powers between men and their
material world on the one hand and God on the other. St. Paul is at
pains to point out, taking their own terms and using them for his
purpose, that, whatever powers one likes to think of in the
universe, above them all towers the Figure of Christ risen and
enthroned, Head of the Church which is His body (vv. 22-23).

Ephesians 3: 14-21

<table>
<tr><td>A.V.</td><td>N.E.B.</td></tr>
<tr><td>14. For this cause I bow my knees unto the Father of our Lord Jesus Christ,</td><td>With this in mind, then, I kneel in prayer to the Father,</td></tr>
<tr><td>15. Of whom the whole family in heaven and earth is named,</td><td>From whom every family in heaven and on earth takes its name,</td></tr>
<tr><td>16. That he would grant you, according to the riches of his glory, to be strengthened with might by his Spirit in the inner man;</td><td>That out of the treasures of his glory he may grant you strength and power through his Spirit in your inner being,</td></tr>
<tr><td>17. That Christ may dwell in your hearts by faith; that ye, being rooted and grounded in love,</td><td>That through faith Christ may dwell in your hearts in love.</td></tr>
<tr><td>18. May be able to comprehend with all saints what is the breadth, and length, and depth, and height;</td><td>With deep roots and firm foundations, may you be strong to grasp, with all God's people, what is the breadth and length and height and depth of the love of Christ,</td></tr>
<tr><td>19. And to know the love of Christ, which passeth knowledge, that ye might be filled with all the fulness of God.</td><td>And to know it, though it is beyond knowledge. So may you attain to fullness of being, the fullness of God himself.</td></tr>
<tr><td>20. Now unto him that is able to do exceeding abundantly above all that we ask or think, according to the power that worketh in us,</td><td>Now to him who is able to do immeasurably more than all we can ask or conceive, by the power which is at work among us,</td></tr>
<tr><td>21. Unto him be glory in the Church by Christ Jesus throughout all ages, world without end. Amen.</td><td>To him be glory in the church and in Christ Jesus from generation to generation evermore! Amen.</td></tr>
</table>

If the prayer in chapter 1 issued out of a hymn of praise, this
prayer issues out of meditation. St. Paul began it back at v. 1 –
'For this cause I Paul, the prisoner of Jesus Christ for you
Gentiles' – he was going to say 'bow my knees unto the Father',
but the mention of the word 'Gentiles' temporarily distracted him,
and off he went as it were at a tangent! Verses 2-13 are a splendid
digression, a meditation which serves as a fruitful background for
the prayer which is to occupy the latter part of this chapter. We
must glance at the digression briefly.

A disclosure, a veritable revelation, has been made to the
Apostle. It is a revelation hitherto undisclosed – what he terms 'the
mystery' ('His secret', v. 3, N.E.B.). It is the birth of a new race, a
race in which the old terminology of Jew and Gentile, so terribly
divisive, so productive of ideas of racial superiority, counts no
more. The Church has been born. The fellowship has been created.

St. Paul marvels at 'the unfathomable riches of Christ' (v. 8) and
at 'the wisdom of God in all its varied forms' (v. 10, N.E.B.),
many-coloured like a jewel which flashes different hues as it is
turned to different lights. He marvels, too, at the miracle of grace
by which this disclosure has been made to *him* of all men. He is
'less than the least of all saints' (v. 8). Is this mock humility? I
doubt it. Rather, it springs partly from the memory of that
persecution of the Christians of which he seems to have been the
chief perpetrator, and partly from his sheer advance in holiness.
For is it not the experience of all saints, that the nearer they draw
to God, the more conscious they become of their own littleness and
of their dependence on God?

It is against that rich background that he 'bows his knees'. We
now turn to the prayer itself, vv. 14-21.

'I bow my knees.' Often the Jews stood to pray. Is this bowing
of the knees a mark of urgency, as the prostration of the body of
Jesus in the Garden of Gethsemane was an outward sign of the
bowing of His will to do the will of the Father?

For purposes of clarity, we may ask of this prayer the same two
questions which we asked of the prayer in chapter 1 – 'To whom
does the Apostle pray?' and 'what does he pray?'

i. *To whom does he pray?* The answer is to 'the Father', as Jesus
had taught His disciples to pray. But the title is elaborated. He is
'the Father, from whom every family in heaven and on earth takes
its name'; or, possibly, 'from whom all fatherhood derives its
name'. Those to whom the letter is addressed comprise scattered
little groups throughout Asia Minor, often weak, always in a

minority, sometimes persecuted, often despised. But they are little
families of the one great Father, infinitely rich in His grace, the
treasuries of which are available to them. This is the God to whom
he prays.

ii. *What does he pray?* The answer is, in a word, that they may be
strengthened (v. 16). If it be asked how this is to happen, practically
all the rest of the prayer, apart from the doxology of vv. 20-21, is
the reply. The rest of v. 16 and most of vv. 17-19 is given to the
elaboration of the *how* of the strengthening for which he prays. Let
us examine this.

(*a*) It will not be by human effort, but by the divine Spirit at
work in their inmost beings (v. 16). The plant does not grow in
beauty and fruitfulness by striving, but rather by openness to the
powers of nature which are available to it and for whose reception
it is made. This is what St. John means by 'abiding in Christ', as
the branch 'abides in' the vine. Separated from the vine, it rapidly
withers and dies. United with the vine, it flourishes and brings
forth fruit (*St. John* 15: 1-7). Of course, there must be constant
watch and prayer. Of course, there must be discipline and the
denial of self. But growth in grace, what is called here 'being
strengthened', is primarily the work of the Spirit. It is *His* fruit
which is love, joy, peace, and so on. It is 'through faith' (v. 17).

(*b*) St. Paul puts this in another way, when he speaks (v. 17) of
Christ dwelling 'in your hearts in love' (N.E.B.). It is perhaps the
nearest phrase in the Pauline vocabulary to that 'abiding in Christ'
which we have just mentioned in St. John's. Of this, the prayer of
humble access in the Holy Communion service speaks when it
prays that, our sinful bodies and souls having been made clean
through Christ's Body and Blood, 'we may evermore dwell in Him,
and He in us'. His mind, our mind; His will, our will; His peace,
our peace; His joy, our joy — this is the intimacy, the strengthening, of union with Christ.

'In love.' Do these words go with the preceding words? The
New English Bible would have us think so. There can only be the
intimacy of communion with Christ where there is love — unlove,
as it were, 'breaks the connection'. Almost the whole of the First
Epistle of St. John is given to the elaboration of this theme. The
Authorised Version, on the other hand, takes the phrase 'in love'
with the succeeding words — 'rooted and grounded in love'. This is
the soil out of which Christian growth comes. The original is
indecisive. Both are true.

(*c*) They will be strong as, roots going down and foundations being made ever firmer, they get to know the love of Christ in its fulness. Here is a pleasant and suggestive mixture of metaphors, the horticultural and the architectural; the country and the town. (It recurs in *Colossians* 2 : 7: 'Be rooted in Him; be built in Him'.) So will they be *strong* (we are back at the fundamental concept of the prayer) — 'strong to grasp . . . what is the breadth and length and height and depth of the love of Christ'. Will they? Yes! Can they? No — it is beyond knowledge! Language fails him; but they will understand if he writes to them about knowing the unknowable, grasping the ungraspable.

But we have omitted one phrase. This knowledge of the love of Christ comes to me 'with all God's people' (N.E.B.), 'with all saints' (Authorised Version). 'The Fellowship', Anderson Scott used to say, 'is the organ of insight.' I do not grow strong in the knowledge of the love of Christ when I isolate myself from God's people, dwelling by myself in self-righteous isolation. 'Christian doctrine knows nothing of an atomistic individualism' (J. S. Whale, *Christian Doctrine*, p. 126). 'Christian experience is always ecclesiastical experience' (*op. cit.*, p. 128). At the end of a profound passage in which St. Paul has been writing about our knowing all that God of His own grace gives us, he says: 'We . . . possess the mind of Christ' (1 *Corinthians* 2: 16). '*We*', you will note; not 'I'. We dare not cut ourselves off from the illumination which comes to us from other Christians — men and women of backgrounds, nationalities, cultures, other than our own; yes, and let it be added with vehemence, from branches of Christ's holy, catholic Church other than our own.

The prayer, then, is a prayer for power — 'to be strengthened with might'. It ends with a doxology (vv. 20-21) to the Lord of Power — to Him who is of power 'to do immeasurably more than all we can ask or conceive, by the power which is at work among us' (N.E.B.). This is what Emerson called 'a sally of love and admiration'. When St. Paul's language soars highest (as in this passage), he is struggling to put into words some tremendous spiritual experience which defies expression. These verses are an attempt to express, in doxological form, the profound truth of the power of Christ available to men, though faith, by His Spirit, in the Church. This is the source at once of his Christian character and of his missionary activity. 'The Spirit of Him that raised up Jesus from the dead' is dwelling in him, giving new life to his mortal body — this is the new principle which transforms life (cp. *Romans* 8: 11). It is, to appropriate some words found at the end of Pope John's

Journal of a Soul (p. 450), 'the humble prayer of a Christian, who thinks of sin but is aware of forgiveness, thinks of death but with a heart that is sure of resurrection, knows the magnitude of his own unworthiness but knows even better the greater magnitude of the Lord's mercy'.

'To Him be glory!'

Ephesians 6: 23-24

A.V.	N.E.B.
23. Peace be to the brethren, and love with faith, from God the Father and the Lord Jesus Christ.	Peace to the brotherhood and love, with faith, from God the Father and the Lord Jesus Christ.
24. Grace be with all them that love our Lord Jesus Christ in sincerity. Amen.	God's grace be with all who love our Lord Jesus Christ, grace and immortality.

The closing two verses of this circular letter are a kind of mixture of the familiar greeting which we have studied in *Romans* 1: 7, and elsewhere ('Grace to you, and peace . . .'), and of the familiar ending ('The grace of our Lord Jesus Christ be with you all . . .' (pp. 117 ff.). But here 'grace and peace' are joined by 'love and faith' – God's four great gifts to 'the brotherhood'. Or is it *faithfulness* rather than *faith*? For the same word can indicate both. For example, in *Galatians* 5: 22, the Apostle is referring not to religious faith, the relationship of a believer to his Lord, but to the mark of Christian character which is faithfulness, reliability, stability. It may well be so here – St. Paul prays for the brotherhood that faithfulness to their Lord which will hold them firm in His service whatever may be the hazards which they have to endure in their discipleship. The very uncertainty as to translation provides us with food for meditation.

The same is true of the concluding words of v. 24. The Authorised Version translates 'in sincerity'; the Revised Version 'in uncorruptness', referring the phrase to the sincerity of the love borne to our Lord Jesus Christ. The New English Bible, following a different Greek reading, couples the word with 'grace' – 'grace and immortality be with all . . .' It must be granted that this is the more usual meaning of the word. 'It refers either to those who love the Lord, and as such are now partakers of the future life, or to the Lord himself, who reigns in immortal glory' (Arndt and Gingrich: *A Greek-English Lexicon of the New Testament and other Early Christian Literature*, p. 125).

THE EPISTLE TO THE
PHILIPPIANS

Philippians 1: 2-5

A.V.	N.E.B.
2. Grace be unto you, and peace, from God our Father, and from the Lord Jesus Christ.	Grace to you and peace from God our Father and the Lord Jesus Christ.
3. I thank my God upon every remembrance of you,	I thank my God whenever I think of you;
4. Always in every prayer of mine for you all making request with joy,	And when I pray for you all, my prayers are always joyful,
5. For your fellowship in the gospel from the first day until now.	Because of the part you have taken in the work of the Gospel from the first day until now.

IF Galatians is the sternest of the Pauline letters, Philippians is the happiest. 'I rejoice; you rejoice', was Bengel's summary of it. The Epistle is remarkable, too, for the great hymn (2: 5-11) on Christ's self-emptying, and for passages of intimate spiritual autobiography – it is as if the Apostle bares his soul to his readers, especially in 3: 4-15, and 4: 10-18. But these matters do not concern us here. We are considering his prayers. They are few and short. What he says to God *about* his readers is so closely inter-woven with what he writes directly *to* them as to make it difficult to say precisely where prayer ends and message begins.

The prayer in v. 2 is identical with that in *Romans* 1: 7 (pp. 95 ff.).

Right at the start he strikes the note of thanksgiving (v. 3) – 'upon every mention of you' (A.V. margin); 'upon all my remembrance of you' (R.V.). That is to say, whenever they are mentioned to him, or he mentions them to others; or whenever he thinks of them. More likely, however, he is thinking, as the following words may well indicate, of that 'mentioning' of them in prayer which we have already noticed in *Romans* 1: 9, and *Ephesians* 1: 16 (see p. 98 and p. 128), and which we shall notice again (e.g. in

1 *Thessalonians* 1:2; 2 *Timothy* 1:3; or *Philemon* 4). Intercession for them is mixed with joy because of that fellowship in the work of the Gospel which Apostle and Philippians have shared from the start of the Church in that city.

'The first day' — what memories came flooding back! The visit to the proud city of Philippi, a Roman colony, 'a little Rome away from Rome'; the visit to the place of prayer outside the city gate, where, by the riverside, the Apostle and his doctor friend, St. Luke, had talked to the women who gathered there, and talked, without doubt, of things of greater importance than the weather; Lydia's conversion, baptism, and warm welcome of the visitors into her house; the spirit-possessed girl; the exorcism; the riot; the imprisonment; the earthquake and the conversion of the jailer; the release from prison, and the public apology by the magistrates and their dignified send-off as Roman citizens; then back to Lydia's house, and the meeting there for the encouragement of the local Christians. What days they were! Could he ever forget them? (*Acts* 16:12-40).

From the first day until now the news had been good and the progress in the things of Christ consistent. The 'fellowship' (v. 5) had been deep and true. (On 'fellowship', see 2 *Corinthians* 13:14, and pp. 120 ff.) The Apostle could not doubt that He who had begun so good a work in them would see it through to completion. Had He not given them the *pledge* of His Holy Spirit? (*Ephesians* 1:14; see p. 128).

Philippians 1: 9-11

A.V.	N.E.B.
9. And this I pray, that your love may abound yet more and more in knowledge and in all judgment;	And this is my prayer, that your love may grow ever richer and richer in knowledge and insight of every kind,
10. That ye may approve things that are excellent; that ye may be sincere and without offence till the day of Christ;	And may thus bring you the gift of true discrimination. Then on the Day of Christ you will be flawless and without blame,
11. Being filled with the fruits of righteousness, which are by Jesus Christ, unto the glory and praise of God.	Reaping the full harvest of righteousness that comes through Jesus Christ, to the glory and praise of God.

Verses 3-5 assured his readers of St. Paul's thankfulness for them and of his confidence in Christ concerning them. But they did not make clear the content of his prayers on their behalf. Verses 9-11 do just that.

First and foremost comes *love*, 'the very bond of peace and of all virtues, without which whosoever liveth is counted dead before God'. We have already noticed St. Paul's stress on love, in the second great prayer in the Epistle to the Ephesians (3: 17; see pp. 134 ff.). Here he reiterates it. Without it there can be no knowledge (of the spiritual kind he has in mind) nor insight.

On 'knowledge' (*epignosis*) see *Ephesians* 1: 17 (and p. 130). Here the word is elaborated by a second which, with the ensuing phrase, conveys the idea of sensitiveness, ability to discern not merely between good and bad but between two goods, or between the really important and the seemingly important.

The ability to discriminate between one's own mixed motives; knowledge of one's *self*, discerning the real reason for one's words and actions as against the false reasons which masquerade as the true, but are actually only excuses for our laziness or deceitfulness or contentment with the second best. 'And this I pray . . . the gift of true discrimination.'

The ability to discriminate – in one's contact with others. Not indeed, please God, in a spirit of judgement or condemnation, but in the spirit of meekness which will help the other man to 'sort himself out' and see himself as God sees him. 'This I pray . . . the gift of true discrimination'.

The ability to discriminate – in the planning of one's time. The day holds more than can possibly be fitted into it. I can, of course, 'take a mad header' at it, and do nothing well, and at the end be exhausted. Or, given the gift of discernment, I can see what really matters and what may well be left, and in serenity of heart and mind attend to the important, living life *sub specie aeternitatis*. 'This I pray . . . the gift of true discrimination.'

All this is with an eye to the Day of Christ (v. 10), 'when the secrets of all hearts shall be disclosed'. We have already noticed the ethical power of the eschatological hope (*Ephesians* 1: 18; see pp. 130 ff.) – the desire to 'be flawless and without blame' (v. 10) on the Day when we know as we are known. Bishop Stephen Neill puts the point well in his book *Christian Holiness*: 'Christians are a holy people, not because they have attained to a certain grade of ethical respectability, but because God Himself has chosen them out from the world, because in Christ they are chosen and elected and beloved. But everywhere it is taken for granted that this election will have ethical results. To put the matter beyond all doubt, Paul prays for his Philippian friends that they may be "*sincere* and *without offence* in the day of Christ; being filled with the fruits of righteousness . . ." These two carefully chosen adjectives express the two aspects of Christian holiness as the result of divine action — inner purity of motive, and outward blamelessness in relation to other men' (pp. 25-26).

Philippians 4: 20

A.V.	N.E.B.
20. Now unto God and our Father be glory for ever and ever. Amen.	To our God and Father be glory for endless ages! Amen.

This is a little doxology of much simpler form than that which ended the second prayer in the Epistle to the Ephesians (3: 20-21; see pp. 135 ff.). It springs naturally, as did the one in the Epistle to the Ephesians, out of sheer gratitude for the truth of which the Apostle has been writing — in this case the magnificence of the divine riches in Christ Jesus available to the Christian disciple (v. 19).

Philippians 4: 23

A.V.	N.E.B.
23. The grace of our Lord Jesus Christ be with you all. Amen.	The grace of our Lord Jesus Christ be with your spirit.

See 2 *Corinthians* 13: 14 (pp. 117 ff.)

THE EPISTLE TO THE
COLOSSIANS

Colossians 1: 2-4

A.V.

N.E.B.

2. Grace be unto you, and peace, from God our Father and the Lord Jesus Christ.

Grace to you and peace from God our Father.

3. We give thanks to God and the Father of our Lord Jesus Christ, praying always for you,

In all our prayers to God, the Father of our Lord Jesus Christ, we thank him for you,

4. Since we heard of your faith in Christ Jesus, and of the love which ye have to all the saints.

Because we have heard of the faith you hold in Christ Jesus, and the love you bear towards all God's people.

THE greeting in v. 2 is a shortened form of that in *Romans* 1: 7 (pp. 95 ff.). Some manuscripts give the identical form of greeting.

Verses 3-4 are virtually a combination of *Philippians* 1:3 (see pp. 137 ff.) and *Ephesians* 1: 15 (see pp. 126 ff.). Both the 'faith' and the 'love' among the Colossians, of which St. Paul has heard with such joy, 'spring from' (v. 5, N.E.B.) hope. On hope, see *Ephesians* 1: 18; and p. 130.

The content of the prayer is not stated in this opening paragraph of the Epistle. For this we have to wait until vv. 9-12, to which we now turn.

Colossians 1: 9-12

A.V.

N.E.B.

9. For this cause we also, since the day we heard it, do not cease to pray for you, and to desire that ye might be filled with the knowledge of his will in all wisdom and spiritual understanding;

For this reason, ever since the day we heard of it, we have not ceased to pray for you. We ask God that you may receive from him all wisdom and spiritual understanding for full insight into his will,

141

A.V.

10. That ye might walk worthy of the Lord unto all pleasing, being fruitful in every good work, and increasing in the knowledge of God;

11. Strengthened with all might, according to his glorious power, unto all patience and longsuffering with joyfulness;

12. Giving thanks unto the Father, which hath made us meet to be partakers of the inheritance of the saints in light.

N.E.B.

So that your manner of life may be worthy of the Lord and entirely pleasing to him. We pray that you may bear fruit in active goodness of every kind, and grow in the knowledge of God.

May he strengthen you, in his glorious might, with ample power to meet whatever comes with fortitude, patience, and joy;

And to give thanks to the Father who has made you fit to share the heritage of God's people in the realm of light.

The prayer is very closely similar to that in *Ephesians* 1: 15 ff. The Apostle's mind moves in the same circle of ideas, and the vocabulary is much the same in both passages — 'knowledge' (*epignosis* — see p. 130) and 'wisdom' and (here is a new word in the New Testament prayers) spiritual 'understanding'. The accent here is on knowledge of the will of God and on a life which carries that knowledge into effect. There is nothing static about such knowledge; there must be constant 'increase' in it (v. 10). 'You will never lead souls heavenward unless climbing yourself. You need not be very far up; but you must be climbing' (Bishop Walsham How).

The prayer of Archbishop William Temple makes the point, and we may well make it our own:

'So fill our minds with the thought and our imaginations with the picture of Thy love, that there may be in us no room for any desire that is discordant with Thy holy will. Cleanse us, we pray Thee, from all that may make us deaf to Thy call or slow to obey it . . .'

This prayer of St. Paul is a prayer for patience and longsuffering and joy (v. 11) — humdrum virtues, as some would say. Archbishop Cosmo Lang once wrote to Canon C. F. Garbett, the future Archbishop of York, then Vicar of Portsea, when Garbett was feeling the weight of his work and of middle age: '. . . chiefly I think the treatment like the malady must be spiritual. A more eager and constant reference of oneself and all one's relationships and activities to the Spirit of God — the Paraclete who inwardly

succours men who are trudging along the flats of middle-age . . .
St. Paul's words in *Colossians* 1: 11, often come home to me —
"strengthened with all power according to the might of His glory"
— *not*, as we might expect from such high endowment, unto all
exaltation and vigour, but — "unto all patience and long-suffering".
All the might of His glory to enable us to be patient — just to hold
on. It is only when this vocation to patience is accepted that we can
pass on to the result — "with joy".' (Charles Smyth, *Cyril Forster
Garbett*, p. 136).

Patience (or staying-power), long-suffering, joy (v. 11), thanksgiving (v. 12) to God for what grace has granted us to be — it is a
shining series; a ladder to glory.

Colossians 4: 3-4

A.V.	N.E.B.
3. Withal praying also for us, that God would open unto us a door of utterance, to speak the mystery of Christ, for which I am also in bonds:	That God may give us an opening for preaching, to tell the secret of Christ; that indeed is why I am now in prison.
4. That I may make it manifest, as I ought to speak.	Pray that I may make the secret plain, as it is my duty to do.

Up till now, in considering the prayers of St. Paul, we have had
before us the prayers which he prayed for his friends. Now we have
a change. He tells them what he wants them to pray for him,
prisoner that he is as a result of having preached the word of God.
Both the language used in the prayer (especially the word
'mystery') and the content of the prayer deserve consideration.
Perhaps I cannot do better than quote what I have elsewhere
written about them:

'The world of the first century into which Christianity was born
was a world in which secret cults abounded. These cults had a
language of their own — their adherents loved to talk of mysteries, and
initiates, and intermediary beings between that world and this world
of evil matter, of light and darkness, of gnosis, "knowledge". Saul of
Tarsus, Jew though he was, grew up in a town where this language
was part of the linguistic coinage in use every day. When, as a
Christian Apostle, he later came to write his letters, he found himself
using the language of the cults. Perhaps such language had become
part of the jargon of the day, in much the same way as certain

scientific terms have become part of our vocabulary though many of us would find it hard to define these terms in such a way as would satisfy the experts. Perhaps he used these terms the better to catch the ear of those whom he wished to reach with his message. Anyhow he used them—and *mysterion*, "mystery", is a case in point. The strange thing, however, is that he used this word not in the context of something hidden for the benefit of initiates only but of something made known for the benefit of all. "It is a particularly pointed paradox", says Professor C. F. D. Moule, "to speak of *mysterion* in connection with *phaneroun* (v. 4) when that verb means (as it does here) a public manifestation". St. Paul's use of the term may be compared to the case of a doctor who, in the course of his work, lights upon a cure for some fell disease; thereafter his only concern is to make known what has hitherto been hidden from the eyes of men.

'It is precisely because St. Paul, in common with all the great writers of the New Testament, believed that the Gospel did provide and offer a cure for man's radical disease of sin and maladjustment with God and his neighbours, that his one consuming passion was to make clear that which, prior to the coming of our Lord Jesus Christ, had been hidden or at best seen only in shadow. To the declaration of that mystery, to the making plain of that good news he devoted all his considerable powers, and for it he eventually died.

'The health of the Church at any given time may, in large part, be judged by the care that she is giving to just this task. Is she making the mystery of Christ plain as she ought to speak? Is that the primary task to which she is bending her energies and for which she is training her best men? Or, on the other hand, is she allowing herself to be side-tracked into other tasks which, however worthy, are contributing more to her own glory than to the magnifying and clarifying of her message? These are questions of fundamental importance. The Church must never allow herself to be deflected from giving her closest attention to them' (*Christian Priorities*, pp. 65-66).

Here is a prayer to be used on behalf of the Church of God as a whole, on behalf of the individual Christian within it, and especially on behalf of those who preach.

Colossians 4: 12

A.V.

12. ... always labouring fervently for you in prayers, that ye may stand perfect and complete in all the will of God.

N.E.B.

... He prays hard for you all the time, that you may stand fast, ripe in conviction and wholly devoted to doing God's will.

Chapter 1 told us what the Apostle prayed for the Colossians. Chapter 4: 3-4, told us what he wanted them to pray for him. This verse tells us what a colleague of the Apostle prays for them, thus giving us an insight into the mind of one of whose Christian service St. Paul thought very highly. Epaphras, though himself coming from Colossae (v. 12), was absent from his friends in body; but

> '. . . though sundered far, by faith they meet
> Around one common mercy-seat.'
>
> (H. Stowell)

He was able to bring to the Apostle news about the Colossians which made him glad (1: 7 ff.).

What does Epaphras pray for his own people? The prayer is short but powerful – that 'you may stand fast' (*stability*); 'ripe in conviction' (*maturity*); 'wholly devoted to doing God's will' (*willing obedience*). If the emphasis of Epaphras' prayer on doing the will of God echoes the Apostle's own emphasis (1: 9-10), that is not to be wondered at. The two men no doubt often meditated together, conversed together, prayed together.

Colossians 4: 18

A.V.	N.E.B.
18. Grace be with you. Amen.	God's grace be with you.

See 2 *Corinthians* 13: 14 (pp. 117 ff.).

THE EPISTLES TO THE
THESSALONIANS

1 Thessalonians 1: 1-5

A.V.

1. Paul, and Silvanus, and Timotheus, unto the church of the Thessalonians which is in God the Father, and in the Lord Jesus Christ: Grace be unto you, and peace, from God our Father, and the Lord Jesus Christ.

2. We give thanks to God always for you all, making mention of you in our prayers;

3. Remembering without ceasing your work of faith, and labour of love, and patience of hope in our Lord Jesus Christ, in the sight of God and our Father;

4. Knowing, brethren beloved, your election of God.

5. For our gospel came not unto you in word only, but also in power, and in the Holy Ghost, and in much assurance; as ye know what manner of men we were among you for your sake.

N.E.B.

From Paul, Silvanus, and Timothy to the congregation of Thessalonians who belong to God the Father and the Lord Jesus Christ. Grace to you and peace.

We always thank God for you all, and mention you in our prayers continually.

We call to mind, before our God and Father, how your faith has shown itself in action, your love in labour, and your hope of our Lord Jesus Christ in fortitude.

We are certain, brothers beloved by God, that he has chosen you

And that when we brought you the Gospel, we brought it not in mere words but in the power of the Holy Spirit, and with strong conviction, as you know well. That is the kind of men we were at Thessalonica, and it was for your sake.

THE greeting is an abbreviated form of that in *Romans* 1: 7 (see pp. 95ff.).

The prayer is one of thanksgiving, based on all the progress made by the Thessalonian Christians since the stormy days of the birth of the Christian community in the city. The story of that beginning, as recorded in the seventeenth chapter of the Acts, is an interesting one. As usual, the Apostle started with the local

synagogue. On three successive Sabbath days, he argued with his
hearers; perhaps *Acts* 17: 3 gives the themes of his three discourses
– first Sabbath, that Messiah had to suffer; second Sabbath, that
Messiah had to rise from the dead; third Sabbath, that this Jesus
whom he was proclaiming was the Messiah. The result of his
preaching and arguing was the establishment of a Christian community, a mixed group of Jews and God-fearing Greeks and
influential women. The result was also a riot, as a consequence of
which the congregation thought it to be the course of wisdom to
send Paul and his companion, Silas, on their way.

Now the years have passed, but not the memories, nor the
prayers. As for his friends at Rome (1: 9) and in the churches in
Asia Minor to whom Ephesians is addressed (1: 16), so for the
Thessalonians – he 'makes mention of them' in his prayers.

The reasons for his thanksgiving are elaborated in v. 3 ff.: *First*,
he sees in the Thessalonian Christians the trinity of graces on
which he often loves to dwell – 'faith, love, and hope' (I quote the
order given here, not that given in 1 *Corinthians* 13: 13). All three
have been productive – faith has shown itself in action, love in
labour, hope in fortitude. The last phrase particularly deserves note.
We have already seen what is uppermost in St. Paul's mind when he
writes of 'hope'(*Ephesians* 1: 18; see pp. 130ff.). Here he states that
it is productive of 'fortitude' (v. 3). The Authorised Version and
the Revised translate the word by 'patience'. But this is altogether
too weak a translation for the powerful word used here. 'Endurance', 'the steady determination to see things through' – this is
what is implicit in the word. We shall come across it again, and
especially in connection with the character of the incarnate Christ
in 2 *Thessalonians* 3: 5 (see p. 158).

Secondly, his reason for thanksgiving is his certitude of their
election by God (v. 4). Election to the Apostle was not so much a
theme for theoretical discussion (perhaps *Romans* 9-11 may be
considered as something of an exception to this statement) as a
cause for thanskgiving –

> ' 'Twas not so much that I on Thee took hold,
>   As Thou, dear Lord, on me.'

What he writes of election springs from a deeply held conviction
that he himself had been grasped (*Philippians* 3: 12) by strong
Hands and turned round in his tracks. What was true of him in
startling fashion was none the less true of the Thessalonian

Christians, even if their conversion had been less dramatic than his own.

Thirdly, his reason for thanksgiving is the power of the Gospel (v. 5). Of course, it had to come to them in words – how else could the message of the crucified and risen Christ be conveyed? But it came not in *mere* words. The words were taken up by the Holy Spirit and, by His power, brought strong conviction. That is why preaching must never be despised. What *is* preaching? A man talking? A man trying to put across his bright ideas? Far from it. Preaching is God the Holy Spirit taking 'mere words' and using them as the medium through which He brings strong conviction resulting in changed lives, evidenced by faith and hope and love. 'Some of them were convinced and joined Paul and Silas; so did a great number of godfearing Greeks and a good many influential women' (*Acts* 17: 4, N.E.B.).

As we make this prayer our own, we may combine with it the following:

'Grant to us, O God—
    the Faith which sees the cross and knows that all men
    may be redeemed:
    the Hope which sees the empty tomb and knows that good
    must triumph over evil:
    the Love which sees Jesus and knows that in Him alone
    the hearts of men can be fully satisfied:
    through the same, Jesus Christ our Lord'.

1 Thessalonians 2: 13

A.V.	N.E.B.
13. For this cause also thank we God without ceasing, because, when ye received the word of God which ye heard of us, ye received it not as the word of men, but as it is in truth, the word of God, which effectually worketh also in you that believe.	This is why we thank God continually, because when we handed on God's message, you received it, not as the word of men, but as what it truly is, the very word of God at work in you who hold the faith.

This short prayer of thanksgiving is an elaboration of the last part of the prayer which we have just considered (1: 5). In it, St. Paul again looks back to the reception accorded to his preaching when he worked in Thessalonica. The verse is reminiscent of the passage in *Romans* 10: 14 ff. 'How could they have faith in one they had never heard of? And how hear without someone to spread the news? And how could anyone spread the news without a commission to do so?' (N.E.B.). He was commissioned. He had spread the news. He had told them of Jesus Christ. And they had 'received it' as the very word of God and, receiving it as such, had found it a power to reckon with in their lives. (The word translated in the Authorised Version 'effectually worketh' is the word we know in English as *energy*.)

What are words? Nothing in themselves. But when they are the medium of the revelation of God's grace, and when they are received in faith, they become power, energy, dynamite.

1 Thessalonians 3: 10-13

A.V.	N.E.B.
10. Night and day praying exceedingly that we might see your face, and might perfect that which is lacking in your faith?	Making us rejoice before our God while we pray most earnestly night and day to be allowed to see you again and to mend your faith where it falls short?
11. Now God himself and our Father, and our Lord Jesus Christ, direct our way unto you.	May our God and Father himself, and our Lord Jesus, bring us direct to you;
12. And the Lord make you to increase and abound in love one toward another, and toward all men, even as we do toward you:	And may the Lord make your love mount and overflow towards one another and towards all, as our love does towards you.
13. To the end he may establish your hearts unblameable in holiness before God, even our Father, at the coming of our Lord Jesus Christ with all his saints.	May he make your hearts firm, so that you may stand before our God and Father holy and faultless when our Lord Jesus comes with all those who are his own.

The prayer of vv. 10-13 issues out of the thankfulness which St. Paul expresses in v. 9 as he looks back to his first visit (cf. 1: 2-5). It comes from a heart which was deeply and devotedly pastoral. He must be a very blind reader of the Pauline letters who cannot trace, through practically all of them, the warmth of affection which the writer has for his readers. Even in the stern letter to the Galatians, they are 'my little children, of whom I travail in birth again until

Christ be formed in you' (4: 19); the runaway slave Onesimus is to be received as 'a brother beloved', 'as myself' (*Philemon* 16, 17); though the Corinthians may have ten thousand tutors, yet they have only one father in Christ, and he is precisely that (1 *Corinthians* 4: 15) – and so on. Deep affection and care, even tenderness, are discernible in the letters. So it is here. He longs to see their face – it is a pity that the New English Bible omits this human touch and translates 'to see you' (v. 10). Faces mirror character. The intervening years between the first visit and the projected visit will have etched lines which will speak of deeper love and saintlier lives. 'We pray that we may see your face.'

There will be gaps in their faith which will need *mending* (v. 10) – we met this concept in 2 *Corinthians* 13: 9 (see pp. 116 ff.), and shall meet it again in *Hebrews* 13: 21 (see p. 169). What does he mean by *faith* here? Their creed, perhaps. He had had only three brief Sabbaths with them, and then there had been the riot and he had had to move on (*Acts* 17: 1-10). There is much that he would like to add, 'unsearchable riches' which he would like to share with them. Or perhaps he was alluding to their *faithfulness*, deficient in certain ways and in need of 'mending'. Perhaps he meant both.

Anyway, may God grant a swift, unhindered meeting (v. 11). We should not fail to note how, in this very early letter (it is usually dated about A.D. 52), it is perfectly natural for the Apostle to bracket' the Person of 'our Lord Jesus Christ' with 'God our Father' (cp. 1 *Corinthians* 8: 6) – already there has been swift and sure development of a high Christology.

Meanwhile, till they meet, what shall he pray for them? Two things: love (v. 12) and holiness (v. 13). *Love* – to one another, of course. But the scope of their love must not end with the fellowship. It must extend 'toward all men', embracing all within its generous grasp. May that kind of love 'increase and abound', 'mount and overflow' – the New English Bible translation makes us think of a rising river which waters a plain.

And *holiness* (v. 13) – more than that, *stable holiness*, as the Psalmist had declared: 'O God, my heart is fixed' (*Psalms* 108: 1) in an unchangeability of purpose. Here, then, must be their goal, and this shall be his prayer for them, that on the great day of the Lord, when Jesus comes with all His saints, they may stand before Him holy and faultless. We note again, the spur of the eschatological hope (cf. pp. 130 ff.).

Love and holiness – what better stars than these to which to hitch the wagon of their prayers?

1 Thessalonians 5: 23

A.V.	N.E.B.
23. And the very God of peace sanctify you wholly; and I pray God your whole spirit and soul and body be preserved blameless unto the coming of our Lord Jesus Christ.	May God himself, the God of peace, make you holy in every part, and keep you sound in spirit, soul, and body, without fault when our Lord Jesus Christ comes.

We may regard this prayer as an elaboration of the one we have just considered (3: 12-13). There is the same accent on holiness. There is the same forward look to the coming of our Lord Jesus Christ. But there are elements not present in the former prayer.

First, it is addressed to 'the God of peace' (cp. *Romans* 1: 7 and 15: 33; see pp. 95 ff. and p. 106).

Secondly, the sphere of operation where holiness is to abound is defined – may they be kept 'sound in spirit, soul, and body'; there is to be no part of their being where the burning, shining holiness of God does not penetrate.

Thirdly, there is at the close of the prayer (v. 24) the assurance of the faithfulness of the God who is constantly calling them to holiness. He will see them through. It is a favourite concept of the Apostle's. We have seen it before (*Ephesians* 1: 14; see p. 128). We find it again, for example, in 1 *Corinthians* 10: 13, where, against the sombre background of Israel's failure, St. Paul warns his readers against self-confidence (v. 12). Temptations will assail the Corinthians as they assailed the Israelites of old. But there is no need to succumb – '*God is faithful*', and He will see them through. So here – holiness in spirit, soul, and body is no mean goal. The obstacles to its attainment are mighty. But – 'God is faithful. He calls. He effects.'

1 Thessalonians 5: 28

A.V.	N.E.B.
28. The grace of our Lord Jesus Christ be with you. Amen.	The grace of our Lord Jesus Christ be with you!

See 2 *Corinthians* 13: 14 (pp. 117 ff.)

2 Thessalonians 1: 2-4

A.V.	N.E.B.

2. Grace unto you, and peace, from God our Father and the Lord Jesus Christ:

Grace to you and peace from God the Father and the Lord Jesus Christ.

3. We are bound to thank God always for you, brethren, as it is meet, because that your faith groweth exceedingly, and the charity of every one of you all toward each other aboundeth;

Our thanks are always due to God for you, brothers. It is right that we should thank him, because your faith increases mightily, and the love you have, each for all and all for each, grows ever greater.

4. So that we ourselves glory in you in the churches of God for your patience and faith in all your persecutions and tribulations that ye endure.

Indeed we boast about you ourselves among the congregations of God's people, because your faith remains so steadfast under all your persecutions, and all the troubles you endure.

The prayer of v. 2 is identical with that of *Romans* 1 : 7 (pp. 95 ff.).

As in the opening prayer of the first Epistle (1 *Thessalonians* 1 : 3), so in this, the cause for St. Paul's thanksgiving is news of the growth and abundance of the Thessalonians' faith and love (v. 3) and — hope? We noted the trinity of graces in the first Epistle (p. 147), and we noted that hope was linked with fortitude. Here, in v. 4, no specific mention is made of the third member of the trinity of graces, but 'fortitude' finds a place. The two prayers are closely parallel.

What was said in the notes on the former passage about 'patience' (or, better, 'endurance', 'steadfastness') is corroborated here. For the word occurs in the context of 'persecutions and troubles' endured by the Thessalonians. What form precisely these took we do not know. But it would not be a wild guess to surmise that the Jews were instrumental, at least in part, in making the lives of the Christians difficult. After all, on St. Paul's visit, it was they who 'recruited some low fellows from the dregs of the populace, roused the rabble, and had the city in an uproar' (*Acts* 17: 5, N.E.B.). It was possible to smuggle the Apostle away; but *they* lived there, and there they had to bear their witness. One's own neighbourhood is always the most difficult place in which to take one's stand as a Christian. St. Paul might be forgiven if, as a father in relation to his children, he did a bit of boasting about the splendid way in which the Macedonians had remained steadfast under all their sufferings.

2 Thessalonians 1: 11-12

A.V.	N.E.B.
11. Wherefore also we pray always for you, that our God would count you worthy of this calling, and fulfil all the good pleasure of his goodness, and the work of faith with power:	With this in mind we pray for you always, that our God may count you worthy of his calling, and mightily bring to fulfilment every good purpose and every act inspired by faith,
12. That the name of our Lord Jesus Christ may be glorified in you, and ye in him, according to the grace of our God and the Lord Jesus Christ.	So that the name of our Lord Jesus may be glorified in you, and you in him, according to the grace of our God and the Lord Jesus Christ.

The dominant note of the opening part of this prayer is that of 'the calling'. What he has in mind is so clear to the Apostle that he has no need to qualify the noun, as does the Authorised Version ('this') and the New English Bible ('his'). It is something specific and unique. In the first Epistle (5: 24), God is entitled 'the One who is calling you'. We have noted the phrase 'the hope of His calling' (*Ephesians* 1: 18; see pp. 130-131). The Apostle, in an autobiographical passage of great significance, speaks of pressing 'towards the goal to win the prize which is God's call to the life above . . .' (*Philippians* 3: 14, N.E.B.). The translation is a free one. The Greek reads simply 'the prize of God's upward calling . . .' The thought is certainly not limited to the life to come, (nor does the translation of the New English Bible *necessarily* imply this). The call operates in the here and now. It is like the call of the mountain to a climber — 'higher, ever higher'. The climber, having mastered a stiff bit of mountaineering, may think that he has reached the summit. But he is wrong. There are further heights ahead of him; and in these heights, waiting to be scaled, there seems to be an imperious summons. It is an 'upward call', and a demanding one.

Such a call has come to the Thessalonians. St. Paul thinks of it in the setting of 'that great Day' (v. 10, N.E.B.). As we have often noticed before, so now we see that the eschatological background to the Apostle's thinking is the only one which enables him to get

his proportions right. Only when the events of *this* world are seen
against the verities of *that* world am I likely to think big and live
big. 'We . . . are citizens of heaven, and from heaven we expect our
deliverer to come', wrote St. Paul to men very proud of their
Roman citizenship (*Philippians* 3: 20, N.E.B.). That is the
measure of 'the calling'!

The prayer goes on (v. 11) that God will 'mightily bring to
fulfilment every good purpose and every act inspired by faith'.
There is to be no stunted growth, no good beginnings and bad
endings. With what in view? The 'glorifying of the name of our
Lord Jesus Christ'. (On 'glory' and 'glorify' see *St. John* 17, and
pp. 63 ff.)

That much is clear. But there is another phrase to the prayer
which must not pass unnoticed – 'so that you (may be glorified) in
Him'. Glorified Christians are those who, 'beholding . . . the glory
of the Lord, are changed into the same image from glory to glory'
(2 *Corinthians* 3: 18).

In a cargo-boat on one of the American lakes, the old negro
engine-man was asked how he kept his engine-room so bright and
shining. He replied: 'Oh! I gotta glory' –

'Oh! you gotta get a glory
In the work you do;
A Hallelujah chorus
In the heart of you.
Paint, or tell a story,
Sing, or shovel coal,
But you gotta get a glory
Or the job lacks soul.

The great, whose shining labours
Make our pulses throb,
Were men who got a glory
In their daily job.
The battle might be gory
And the odds unfair,
But the men who got a glory
Never knew despair.

Oh, Lord, give me a glory,
When all else is gone!
If you've only got a glory
You can still go on.'

2 Thessalonians 2: 13-14

A.V.

N.E.B.

13. But we are bound to give thanks always to God for you, brethren beloved of the Lord, because God hath from the beginning chosen you to salvation through sanctification of the Spirit and belief of the truth:

But we are bound to thank God for you, brothers beloved by the Lord, because from the beginning of time God chose you to find salvation in the Spirit that consecrates you, and in the truth that you believe.

14. Whereunto he called you by our gospel, to the obtaining of the glory of our Lord Jesus Christ.

It was for this that he called you through the gospel we brought, so that you might possess for your own the splendour of our Lord Jesus Christ.

These verses give the content of the prayer of thanksgiving which the Apostle offers when he thinks of the Thessalonians. God's *choice* of them (v. 13), His *call* of them (v. 14), results in salvation (v. 13) and in the possession for their own of the glory, the splendour, of our Lord Jesus Christ (v. 14).

The salvation of which he speaks is fulness of life here and hereafter. It is life freed from those restrictions which sin imposes. The writer explains where this freedom is to be found. It is found, *first*, 'in the Spirit that consecrates you'. That is to say, there is available to the Christian a source of power which makes for righteousness and holiness. The Pentecostal gift is a gift which makes a man like Jesus. It is 'the divine power which may be in conflict with man but purposes to sanctify him in his entirety' (A. M. Ramsey, *Sacred and Secular*, p. 20). But it is not automatic. For, *secondly*, it is found 'in the truth that you believe'. That truth must be received. It must be assimilated. It must be wrestled with. It must be digested, if the powers available through the Spirit are to be made use of. That way comes salvation. That way comes 'glory' (see 2 *Thessalonians* 1: 12).

2 Thessalonians 2: 16-17

A.V.

N.E.B.

16. Now our Lord Jesus Christ himself, and God, even our Father, which hath loved us, and hath given us everlasting consolation and good hope through grace,

And may our Lord Jesus Christ himself and God our Father, who has shown us such love, and in his grace has given us such unfailing encouragement and such bright hopes,

A.V.   N.E.B.

17. Comfort your hearts, and   Still encourage and fortify you in
stablish you in every good word   every good deed and word!
and work.

The thanksgiving at the thought of the Thessalonians in vv. 13-14
gives place to a prayer for them. It is a prayer for encouragement
and for fortifying.

On encouragement, inadequately translated in the Authorised
Version by 'consolation', see *Romans* 15: 5; pp. 102 ff. Perhaps the
idea of comfort is present here – no doubt the Thessalonians had
troubles enough. This is an authentic element in the rich verb used
here; and we have noted it in such a passage as 2 *Corinthians* 1: 2-4.
But the New English Bible is undoubtedly right in giving us the
more positive translation 'encouragement' here, as so often elsewhere in the New Testament. The noun not only looks back,
where consolation is needed for what is past, but forward where
stimulation is needed for the future.

The second of the two verbs used in v. 17 (A.V. 'stablish',
N.E.B. 'fortify') has an element of the immovable about it. It is
used of a chasm *fixed* (*St. Luke* 16: 26); of a face *set* in determination (*St. Luke* 9: 51). Though the word used in 1 *Corinthians*
15: 58, is different, the thought is very similar – Christians are to
be *immovable*, abounding in the work of the Lord.

This stimulation and encouragement will take place in the realm
of the *heart* (v. 17). That, to a Hebrew like St. Paul, meant not
merely the seat of the emotions but of the determinative *will*,
where self is dethroned and 'where Jesus reigns alone'. This is
elaborated in the latter part of this verse, where the 'fortifying'
works out in the sphere of 'every good word and work', his words
and work being the two main ways by which a man expresses what
is within him.

We may, finally, notice to whom the prayer is addressed. It is to
'our Lord Jesus Christ himself and God our Father' – again we
notice the juxtaposition even in this early letter when 'Christology'
as such had had little time to develop. The Throne of deity is a
shared Throne! (See p. 150.)

The address is elaborated. This God is the God 'which hath
loved us'. It is probable that the tense used here is a timeless one –
it has no bounds or horizons to it (it is an *aorist*). Or it may refer
back to an event – *the* event which was the supreme manifestation
of the eternal love of God, namely, the cross. Further, He is the

God 'who hath given us everlasting consolation and good hope through grace'. 'Consolation' is the noun which derives from the verb which we have just been examining in v. 17 and which we have translated by 'encourage' or 'stimulate' or a mixture of both! 'Hope' is again a familiar concept. It may be doubted whether the New English Bible translation 'such bright hopes' is adequate. The Greek is singular, not plural. Is not St. Paul here referring to one hope above all others, using the word as we have several times previously noticed him use it, in the sense of the restoration of the image of God in us which has been defaced by sin (e.g. *Ephesians* 1: 18)? *This* is the Christian hope *par excellence*. With *this* in view —

'. . . hearts are brave again, and arms are strong.
Alleluia!'

2 Thessalonians 3: 1-2

A.V.	N.E.B.
1. Finally, brethren, pray for us, that the word of the Lord may have free course, and be glorified, even as it is with you:	And now, brothers, pray for us, that the word of the Lord may have everywhere the swift and glorious course that it has had among you,
2. And that we may be delivered from unreasonable and wicked men: for all men have not faith.	And that we may be rescued from wrong-headed and wicked men; for it is not all who have faith.

The closing verses of chapter 2 record St. Paul's prayer for the Thessalonians. The opening verses of chapter 3 record what he wants them to pray for him and his companions. It is a prayer *first* for a 'swift and glorious course' for 'the word of the Lord', and *secondly* (and only then) for personal deliverance. Whatever happens to him and his party, the word of the Lord must 'run', unhindered, for, where the word 'runs', life comes as it had done in Thessalonica.

But it may well be that the two requests are not wholly unconnected. If the little Pauline company become the victims of 'wrong-headed and wicked men', then there will very likely be a setback to the progress of the word of the Lord. We have seen this happen all too frequently in Communist-dominated countries.

The word translated 'unreasonable' (A.V.), 'wrong-headed' (N.E.B.), is only used elsewhere in the New Testament of *things*;

in *St. Luke* 23: 41, 'this man hath done nothing amiss', out of place, wrong; and in *Acts* 25: 5, 'if there is anything wrong' in the man (Paul), 'let them prosecute him' (N.E.B.). There may be a suggestion, in the use of the word in this prayer, that the men whom St. Paul has in mind are where they ought not to be, standing in the way of the word of the Lord, hindering it from having its free and glorious course.

2 Thessalonians 3: 5

A.V.	N.E.B.
5. And the Lord direct your hearts into the love of God, and into the patient waiting for Christ.	May the Lord direct your hearts towards God's love and the steadfastness of Christ!

No deflection – that is the burden of this prayer. No turning to the right hand nor to the left. 'Let thine eyes look right on and thine eye-lids ever before thee' – right on to God's love and Christ's steadfastness.

'The love of God' – what does that mean? 'Our love for God' – let nothing distract us from that? Possibly. But more likely 'the love that God has for us' – let that be ever in our thoughts.

'And the steadfastness of Christ' (N.E.B.). Not, as in the Authorised Version, 'the patient waiting for Christ'. The Apostle is not here thinking of the coming of Christ in glory. He is thinking of His first coming in humility and what it was that characterised Him then. It was the steadfastness of Him who endured the contradiction of sinners against Himself; who, when He could see little return for it, loved His disciples to the uttermost (*St. John* 13: 1). It was refusal to give up. It was determination to plod on, to stick it through, whatever the odds (see *Romans* 15: 5; and pp. 102 ff.). It was staying power.

'The moral laws of endurance, patience, fortitude, and self-discipline are the foundation upon which the Christian graces rest, and without them Christianity itself becomes a sentiment' (G. Goyder, *The People's Church*, p. 64).

When hearts (i.e. wills, see 2: 17) are thus directed, Christian character grows and Christian witness is clear.

2 Thessalonians 3: 16

A.V.	N.E.B.
16. Now the Lord of peace himself give you peace always by all means. The Lord be with you all.	May the Lord of peace himself give you peace at all times and in all ways. The Lord be with you all.

On the similar phrase 'the God of peace, see *Romans* 1 : 7 and 15: 33 (see pp. 95 ff. and p. 106). The Apostle prays, not merely for the peace of the Lord, but for the Lord Himself to be with them. There can be no peace apart from the Lord of peace. The story is told of St. Thomas Aquinas, that, praying in ecstasy before the image of Christ on the cross, he heard the words: 'Thomas, you have written well about Me; what reward do you want?' To which Thomas replied: 'None other than yourself, Lord' (Hilda Graef, *The Story of Mysticism*, p. 166).

'Always' (A.V.); 'at all times' (N.E.B.). The original means simply 'through all', through all time or through every circumstance. The preposition 'through' is suggestive. The peace of the Lord is not to be found by evading difficulties, but by finding the Lord of peace in the very heart of them. 'When thou passest *through* the waters, I will be with thee.'

'By all means' (A.V.); 'in all ways' (N.E.B.). God has many avenues along which His peace can find its way into a disciple's heart. He is never outwitted. Only our folly can block the coming of the peace of the Lord and of the Lord of peace.

2 Thessalonians 3: 18

A.V.	N.E.B.
18. The grace of our Lord Jesus Christ be with you all. Amen.	The grace of our Lord Jesus Christ be with you all.

See 2 *Corinthians* 13: 14 (pp. 117 ff.)

THE EPISTLES TO TIMOTHY AND TITUS

1 Timothy 1: 2

A.V.	N.E.B.
2. Grace, mercy, and peace, from God our Father and Jesus Christ our Lord.	Grace, mercy, and peace to you from God the Father and Christ Jesus our Lord.

THIS is the introductory greeting which has become so familiar to us in the Pauline Epistles – 'grace and peace . . .' – but with the addition of the word 'mercy', a word which hitherto has only occurred in what is half a goodwill wish and half a prayer, *Galatians* 6: 16. It is a favourite word in the Pastoral Epistles, as 1 and 2 Timothy and Titus are called. We shall meet it again also in *Jude* 2.

In the New Testament, this word 'mercy' is used especially of the mercy shown to men by God in Christ, the God who, as St. Paul puts it in *Ephesians* 2: 4, is 'rich in mercy'. Christians are those who realise that they have a throne of grace, to which they may come with boldness, there to '*obtain mercy*, and find grace to help in time of need' (*Hebrews* 4: 16).

'Mercy' is clearly a very close cousin to 'grace', but the familiar twofold greeting is enriched by its addition.

1 Timothy 1: 12

A.V.	N.E.B.
12. And I thank Christ Jesus our Lord, who hath enabled me, for that he counted me faithful, putting me into the ministry.	I thank him who has made me equal to the task, Christ Jesus our Lord; I thank him for judging me worthy of this trust and appointing me to his service.

If this cannot strictly be called a prayer, it is a statement on the part of the writer for which in fact he gives thanks to God. In *Ephesians* 3: 8, St. Paul expresses his astonishment that, to him of all people, the ministry should have been committed. Here the cause of thanksgiving is the power which is available for the task.

Not only did Christ count him trustworthy (vv. 11-12); not only did He appoint him to His service – him who had treated the Lord so outrageously; but He also made him 'equal to the task' (N.E.B.), 'enabled' him (A.V. and R.V.). The word is that from which we derive the word *dynamic*. A ministry, and divine dynamic for its fulfilment – no wonder that he thanks his Lord!

1 Timothy 1: 17

A.V.	N.E.B.
17. Now unto the King eternal, immortal, invisible, the only wise God, be honour and glory for ever and ever. Amen.	Now to the King of all worlds, immortal, invisible, the only God, be honour and glory for ever and ever! Amen.

As we have noticed elsewhere, meditation on God's great acts of mercy in Christ leads on to doxology, and here we are given one of the most majestic in the New Testament. The description of God given in 6: 15-16, ending with a brief doxology, is similar, though longer and richer. The form of this doxology is thought to be liturgical. 'The King of the ages' is a title of God found in Jewish worship, and points to the unchangeable character of God. Years pass and we change. God is changeless. He is incorruptible, immortal. Unseen, He is alone in the majesty of His eternal being. To such a One we offer worship – 'to Him be honour and glory for ever and ever'.

On *Amen* see p. 41.

1 Timothy 6: 16

A.V.	N.E.B.
16. . . . to whom be honour and power everlasting. Amen.	. . . To him be honour and might for ever! Amen.

See 1 *Timothy* 1: 17 (above)

1 Timothy 6: 21

A.V.	N.E.B.
21. Grace be with thee. Amen.	Grace be with you all!

See 2 *Corinthians* 13: 14 (pp. 117 ff.)

2 Timothy 1: 2-3

A.V.	N.E.B.
2. Grace, mercy, and peace, from God the Father and Christ Jesus our Lord.	Grace, mercy, and peace to you from God the Father and our Lord Jesus Christ.
3. I thank God, whom I serve from my forefathers with pure conscience, that without ceasing I have remembrance of thee in my prayers night and day.	I thank God—whom I, like my forefathers, worship with a pure intention—when I mention you in my prayers; this I do constantly night and day.

The prayer of greeting is identical with that of 1 *Timothy* 1: 2 (p. 160).

The recollection of Timothy on the part of the writer makes him thank God for him. The Revised Version takes 'night and day' with 'longing to see thee'; but the Authorised Version and the New English Bible take it with the reference to prayer—'. . . when I mention you in my prayers; this I do constantly night and day'. On this typically Pauline idea of mentioning people in prayer, see *Romans* 1: 9 (p. 98); *Ephesians* 1: 16; *Philippians* 1: 3; 1 *Thessalonians* 1: 2; and *Philemon* 4.

The phrase 'night and day' may well be much more than a mere manner of speech. It may reflect the experience of sleepless nights —in prison, or on ship, or in pain—when what might have been wasted hours of frustration were used in the fruitful activity of intercessory prayer. Many an invalid could comment on this phrase with a spiritual understanding denied to those whose nights are spent in deep sleep after exhausting days.

2 Timothy 1: 16-18

A.V.	N.E.B.
16. The Lord give mercy unto the house of Onesiphorus; for he oft refreshed me, and was not ashamed of my chains :	But may the Lord's mercy rest on the house of Onesiphorus! He has often relieved me in my troubles. He was not ashamed to visit a prisoner,
17. But, when he was in Rome, he sought me out very diligently, and found me.	But took pains to search me out when he came to Rome, and found me.
18. The Lord grant unto him that he may find mercy of the Lord in that day . . .	I pray that the Lord may grant him to find mercy from the Lord on the great Day . . .

From the New Testament, as little is known of Onesiphorus as is
known of Alexander the copper-smith (4: 14), except that the
former had a 'household' (4: 19). But the second-century *Acts of
Paul and Thecla* states that he had been a citizen of Iconium who,
with his wife Lectra, entertained St. Paul on his first missionary
journey and was converted through him.

From the very few words devoted to him, we get an extra-
ordinarily clear picture of what he did and of what his action
meant to the writer. He tracked him down in Rome — we can
picture the maze of narrow streets and the anxious enquiries. He
found him. He visited him, prisoner though he was. That called for
courage, and Onesiphorus was not lacking in that virtue. Those
visits meant much. 'He braced his morale with his fellowship'
(J. N. D. Kelly, *The Pastoral Epistles*, p. 170).

No wonder that a blessing is called down on his household (had
Onesiphorus himself already died?), and a greeting sent to them
(4: 19)!

2 Timothy 4: 14-16

A.V.	N.E.B.
14. Alexander the coppersmith did me much evil: the Lord reward him according to his works:	Alexander the copper-smith did me a great deal of harm. Retribution will fall upon him from the Lord.
15. Of whom be thou ware also; for he hath greatly withstood our words.	You had better be on your guard against him too, for he violently opposed everything I said.
16. At my first answer no man stood with me, but all men forsook me: I pray God that it may not be laid to their charge.	At the first hearing of my case no one came into court to support me; they all left me in the lurch; I pray that it may not be held against them.

In the Authorised Version, v. 14 is a prayer. Not so in the Revised
Version nor in the New English Bible, both of which, following the
better reading in the Greek, render it as a statement of fact — 'the
Lord will render to him according to his works' (R.V.); 'retribution
will fall upon him . . .' (N.E.B.). Here, then, is no prayer for
retribution. Rather, we have a simple statement of solemn fact — a
man cannot touch one of God's servants for ill, and go unpunished.

To persecute the Church is to persecute Christ (*Acts* 9: 5; see p. 83).

If the verse were taken, according to the poorer rendering, as a prayer for vengeance, it would be out of keeping with v. 16, where the writer prays – as his Master (*St. Luke* 23: 34; and see pp. 53 ff.) and the first martyr of the Christian Church (*Acts* 7: 60; and see pp. 80 ff.) had done before him, that those who had dealt ill with him might not suffer for it.

Imprecation is sub-Christian. Judgement is best left to the Lord (see *Romans* 12: 19 – 'Never take vengeance into your own hands . . .: stand back and let God punish if He will. For it is written: Vengeance belongeth unto Me: I will recompense' (Phillips).

2 Timothy 4: 18

A.V.	N.E.B.
18. . . . To whom be glory for ever and ever. Amen.	. . . Glory to him for ever and ever! Amen.

See 1 *Timothy* 1 : 17 and 6 : 16 (p. 161)

2 Timothy 4: 22

A.V.	N.E.B.
22. The Lord Jesus Christ be with thy spirit. Grace be with you. Amen.	The Lord be with your spirit. Grace be with you all!

This greeting is very like the familiar ending to so many Epistles (see 2 *Corinthians* 13: 14; and pp. 117 ff.); but instead of 'the grace of our Lord Jesus Christ be with you', the greeting is divided into two parts – 'the Lord . . . Grace . . .' Possibly the division helps to personify the greeting, and to stress that grace cannot be conceived of as something in itself. The Giver comes before the gift.

Titus 1: 4

A.V.	N.E.B.
4. Grace, mercy, and peace, from God the Father and the Lord Jesus Christ our Saviour.	Grace and peace from God our Father and Christ Jesus our Saviour.

The greeting is almost identical with that with which the other two Pastoral Epistles begin (1 *Timothy* 1 : 2 and 2 *Timothy* 1 : 2). 'Mercy' is lacking in the best manuscripts. 'Saviour' is substituted for 'Lord' in the title of Christ Jesus.

Titus 3: 15

A.V.	N.E.B.
15. Grace be with you all. Amen.	Grace be with you all!

See 2 *Corinthians* 13 : 14 (pp. 117 ff.)

THE EPISTLE TO PHILEMON

Philemon 3-6

A.V.	N.E.B.
3. Grace to you, and peace, from God our Father and the Lord Jesus Christ.	Grace to you and peace from God our Father and the Lord Jesus Christ.
4. I thank my God, making mention of thee always in my prayers,	I thank my God always when I mention you in my prayers,
5. Hearing of thy love and faith, which thou hast toward the Lord Jesus, and toward all saints;	For I hear of your love and faith towards the Lord Jesus and towards all God's people.
6. That the communication of thy faith may become effectual by the acknowledging of every good thing which is in you in Christ Jesus.	My prayer is that your fellowship with us in our common faith may deepen the understanding of all the blessings that our union with Christ brings us.

VERSE 3 is identical with *Romans* 1: 7 (pp. 95 ff.).
On v. 4 see *Romans* 1: 9 (pp. 98 ff.).
On v. 5 see *Ephesians* 1: 15 (pp. 126 ff.) and *Colossians* 1: 4.
Verse 6 gives us the content of the prayer which St. Paul prays for Philemon, for his little family (was Apphia Philemon's wife and Archippus his son?), and for the congregation of the faithful who met at his house (v. 2). He writes as a 'prisoner' (v. 9); that fact should appeal to Philemon's compassion. And as an 'ambassador' of Christ; that should be a reminder of his authority. He writes as one to whom Philemon owes his very self (v. 19) – had not the Apostle been the means of Philemon's conversion to Christ? Since he went to prison, St. Paul had 'begotten' a son! Onesimus – the Apostle enjoys the pun on his name which means 'useful', 'profitable' – having run away from Philemon has come under the Apostle's care. He is sending him back, and this little letter ('the most gentlemanly of all the Pauline letters') is his commendatory note. There must be a kindly reception for Onesimus – no recriminations, please! He must be treated as a fellow-Christian, for that precisely is what he is. If there has been financial loss, then

the Apostle will make that good. He hopes to pay a personal visit
shortly—a telling point; there is no getting round that one!

Now, against that background, on what should we expect St.
Paul to lay stress? 'Fellowship', of course. That is just what we do
find—'your fellowship with us' (v. 6). We have seen something of
the meaning of Christian fellowship, in 2 *Corinthians* 13: 14 (see
pp. 120 ff.) and elsewhere. Here must be an instance of it worked
out in life. St. Paul was in the fellowship; Philemon had joined
him; but so, now, had Onesimus. They were, despite their very
different backgrounds, brothers in Christ. Then, 'let that fellowship of faith become powerful in the knowledge' (*epignosis*, see
Ephesians 1: 17, and pp. 130 ff.), 'the understanding of all the
blessings which our union with Christ brings us'. It is a prayer
closely related to the actual situation in which Philemon found
himself. In the answering of it, he could have—he must have—a
big share. How could he refuse to do his part?

Philemon 25

A.V.	N.E.B.
25. The grace of our Lord Jesus Christ be with your spirit. Amen.	The grace of the Lord Jesus Christ be with your spirit!

See 2 *Corinthians* 13 : 14 (pp. 117 ff.)

THE EPISTLE TO THE HEBREWS

Hebrews 13: 20-21

A.V.	N.E.B.
20. Now the God of peace, that brought again from the dead our Lord Jesus, that great shepherd of the sheep, through the blood of the everlasting covenant,	May the God of peace, who brought up from the dead our Lord Jesus, the great Shepherd of the sheep, by the blood of the eternal covenant,
21. Make you perfect in every good work to do his will, working in you that which is well-pleasing in his sight, through Jesus Christ; to whom be glory for ever and ever. Amen.	Make you perfect in all goodness so that you may do his will, and may he make of us what he would have us be through Jesus Christ, to whom be glory for ever and ever! Amen.

ON 'the God of peace', see *Romans* 1: 7 and 15: 33 (pp. 95 ff. and 105, and cf. 2 *Thessalonians* 3: 16). Here the title is elaborated. The God of peace is the God of power, for it was He 'who brought up from the dead our Lord Jesus'. Just as in Old Testament days, the supreme manifestation of God's power was seen in His bringing up His people from the living death of Egypt, so now His power is to be seen in the resurrection of Jesus Christ from the dead.

The title 'our Lord Jesus' is also elaborated. He is 'the great Shepherd of the sheep'. Not 'the good Shepherd' – 'the beautiful Shepherd' – as in *St. John* 10: 11, 14, but the *great* One, from whom all true shepherding derives, and from whom come both its authority and its pattern. The great Shepherd's work was costly. It was achieved at the price of blood. The eternal covenant – the new covenant of *St. Matthew* 26: 28, as contrasted with the old Mosaic covenant – was a covenant 'in My blood' (*St. Luke* 22: 20). The good Shepherd of St. John, the great Shepherd of this Epistle, 'lays down His life for the sheep' (*St. John* 10: 15).

There is much packed into this introductory verse. It fastens our attention on the God to whom the prayer is made. Now what is the prayer itself? There is essentially only one request – the New English Bible rendering makes it appear that there are two requests. It is that God will 'make' the readers 'perfect'. All the rest of the elaborate verse is amplification – 'with a view to doing His will' (the *purpose* of the perfecting), 'working in you . . .' (the *means* of the perfecting), 'to whom be glory . . .' (a little doxology).

'Make you perfect.' The word could, more crudely, be translated 'mend you'. We have met it before (2 *Corinthians* 13: 9, and 1 *Thessalonians* 3: 10) and noted that it can be used of mending the holes in fishing nets (*St. Mark* 1: 19) and of mending broken bones (though this usage does not occur in the New Testament). Here the writer presumably has in mind the deficiencies of Christian character and activity, the things which mar the Church's witness, the 'blind spots' which are a stumbling-block to belief on the part of the non-Christian observer. 'May God.mend you, make you whole', so that you may carry out His will as it impinges on society.

It is a great prayer. But for most of us the deficiencies are many and great. The holes in the nets of our service are big. Some of our bones are broken, and we limp haltingly along the Christian way. How be mended? How be made perfect? It will not be simply by a little more human effort, a little more struggle, a little more pulling up of ourselves by our own bootstraps. The God of peace, who is the God of power, has His own resources available for us. *He* will 'work in us'. We set the sail of our will; He fills it with the wind of His Spirit. The thought of St. Paul in *Philippians* 2: 12-13, is similar. He exhorts his readers to 'work out their own salvation . . .' But he cannot leave it at that. That by itself might lead to the barrenness of mere human effort. 'It is God', he says, 'who works in you, inspiring both the will and the deed . . .' (N.E.B.). In fact, as the writer of our Epistle to the Hebrews says in this very prayer, it is all 'through Jesus Christ'. His grace, His risen power, His abiding presence – these, operative in the Christian disciple, enable him to do the will of God.

No wonder the prayer ends with a doxology!

> 'Lord, mend or rather make us; one creation
>   Will not suffice our turn;
> Except Thou make us dayly, we shall spurn
>   Our own salvation.'
>
> (George Herbert, *The Church*)

Hebrews 13: 25

A.V.	N.E.B.
25. Grace be with you all. Amen.	God's grace be with you all!

A singularly short form of The Grace. In the original, 'grace' (or 'the grace') stands alone and unqualified. The addition of the word 'God's' in the New English Bible is in the interests of clarity.

See 2 *Corinthians* 13: 14 (pp. 117 ff.).

THE EPISTLES OF PETER

1 Peter 1: 2

A.V.

N.E.B.

2. Grace unto you, and peace, be multiplied.

Grace and peace to you in fullest measure.

THE familiar greeting with the addition of 'be multiplied' (A.V.), 'in fullest measure' (N.E.B.). See 2 *Peter* 1: 2 (p. 173). The greeting forms a kind of preface to the 'eulogy' which begins at v. 3. As it is just that – a eulogy of God, and not a prayer to Him – we cannot consider it here. We can only note that it provides the key to the understanding of the whole Epistle, for it strikes the note of thanksgiving for the resurrection of Christ, itself a 'cause for great joy' (v. 6, N.E.B.) to Christians undergoing tribulation and persecution for His name.

1 Peter 4: 11

A.V.

N.E.B.

11. . . . to whom be praise and dominion for ever and ever. Amen.

. . . to him belong glory and power for ever and ever. Amen.

This is a statement of fact, as the New English Bible translation makes clear. But it is more than that, for the 'Amen' adds a kind of liturgical note to it, and almost turns it into a prayer. Perhaps it is best to call it an ascription, such as occurs in very closely similar form in 1 *Timothy* 1: 17; 6: 16; and 2 *Timothy* 4: 18. Cp. also 1 *Peter* 5: 11 and 2 *Peter* 3: 18 (though here, in the original, no verb is actually expressed).

1 Peter 5: 10-11

A.V.

N.E.B.

10. But the God of all grace, who hath called us unto his eternal glory by Christ Jesus, after that ye have suffered a while, make you

And the God of all grace, who called you into his eternal glory in Christ, will himself, after your brief suffering, restore, establish,

A.V.	N.E.B.
perfect, stablish, strengthen, settle you.	and strengthen you on a firm foundation.
11. To him be glory and dominion for ever and ever. Amen.	He holds dominion for ever and ever. Amen.

The Authorised Version, possibly influenced by the fact that these two verses end with an 'Amen', reads this as a prayer. The New English Bible, more correctly, takes it as a statement of fact – 'the God of all grace . . . will Himself . . . restore . . .' Statement of fact and prayer are not removed far from one another, and we may legitimately consider this as one of the prayers of the New Testament.

It is a fine prayer, one that we shall do well frequently to make our own. There is a two-fold description of God. *First*, He is 'the God of all grace'. There is little doubt that the word 'grace' had much the same connotation for St. Peter as it had for St. Paul (see 2 *Corinthians* 13: 14; pp. 117 ff.). *Secondly*, He is the One 'who called you into His eternal glory in Christ'. That is to say, the Christian God is not only the God of infinite succour (grace) but also of demand. He calls – He looks for obedience and response. When He speaks, men must answer, or else they will miss that for which they were destined, namely, 'glory'. We have seen before that 'glory' is the restoration of the divine image in which man was made. 'The hope of glory' (*Romans* 5: 2) is the hope that 'we shall be like Him, for we shall see Him as He is' (1 *John* 3: 2). It is to this that He has called us.

The reference to suffering ('after your brief suffering') picks up a major theme of this Epistle. The readers were smarting under trials of many kinds (1: 6); they were suffering for the name of Christ, and the ordeal was fiery (4: 12-16). But however long-drawn-out the ordeal might seem to be, looked at in the light of eternity it was 'brief'. The idea is elaborated by St. Paul in 2 *Corinthians* 4: 17-18.

Four strong verbs of promise round off the statement or prayer. (The New English Bible translation makes it look as if there were only three verbs; but, in fact, 'on a firm foundation' is a somewhat free paraphrase for the fourth verb.) God will 'mend' them. (On the meaning of this, the first verb, see *Hebrews* 13: 21 and note.) The last three verbs cannot well be differentiated from one another in precise meaning, except that the last conveys the idea of a building whose foundations are unshakeable. The over-all effect of the four verbs is to give the impression of a Christian character so firmly founded as to be steadfast and unmoveable in the things of God (1 *Corinthians* 15: 58).

On v. 11, see 1 *Peter* 4: 11; p. 171.

1 Peter 5: 14

A.V.	N.E.B.
14. Peace be with you all that are in Christ Jesus. Amen.	Peace to you all who belong to Christ!

The final greeting is not the usual 'grace', but 'peace', as in 3 *John* 14. On the meaning of 'peace', see *Romans* 1: 7; and pp. 95 ff.

2 Peter 1: 2

A.V.	N.E.B.
2. Grace and peace be multiplied unto you through the knowledge of God, and of Jesus our Lord.	Grace and peace be yours in fullest measure, through the knowledge of God and Jesus our Lord.

The familiar greeting of grace and peace has the addition here of a verb, 'be multiplied unto you' (A.V.), 'be yours in fullest measure' (N.E.B.). It adds warmth to the prayer.

Further, a phrase is added to show how this will take place. It will be 'through the knowledge of God and Jesus our Lord'. 'Knowledge' – it is the *experiential* form of the word which we noticed in the prayers of St. Paul (see especially *Ephesians* 1: 17 and p. 130; and *Philemon* 6).

2 Peter 3: 18

A.V.	N.E.B.
18. To him be glory both now and for ever. Amen.	To him be glory now and for all eternity!

See 1 *Peter* 4: 11 (p. 171)

THE EPISTLES OF JOHN

2 John 3

<table>
<tr><td>A.V.</td><td>N.E.B.</td></tr>
<tr><td>3. Grace be with you, mercy, and peace, from God the Father, and from the Lord Jesus Christ, the Son of the Father, in truth and love.</td><td>Grace, mercy, and peace shall be with us from God the Father and from Jesus Christ the Son of the Father, in truth and love.</td></tr>
</table>

I N the Authorised Version, this verse appears as a prayer – 'grace be with you . . .' though the margin points out what is indeed the case that the Greek is 'shall be . . .' The New English Bible follows the Greek correctly, taking this as a statement of comfort and assurance. No comment, therefore, is called for in a book on the *prayers* of the New Testament.

3 John 2

<table>
<tr><td>A.V.</td><td>N.E.B.</td></tr>
<tr><td>2. Beloved, I wish above all things that thou mayest prosper and be in health, even as thy soul prospereth.</td><td>My dear Gaius, I pray that you may enjoy good health, and that all may go well with you, as I know it goes well with your soul.</td></tr>
</table>

This friendly little letter is addressed to one Gaius, of whom we know nothing except what we can derive from this letter. It is unlikely that he is the same as any of those who bear that name and are mentioned in the Acts and in the Epistles of St. Paul, for Gaius was a common name in the world of the first Christian century.

Here is a simple prayer for physical health and prosperity to match the spiritual well-being of Gaius. Of this well-being the writer has heard through friends (v. 3). Loyalty and kindness (vv. 5-6) have marked his actions. The news has brought deep satisfaction to St. John, the spiritual father of Gaius and his circle (v. 4).

This Johannine prayer for *total* well-being may be compared with the Pauline one for the Thessalonians (1 *Thessalonians* 5: 23; see p. 151), for soundness in spirit, soul and body. To neglect or disparage the physical is no true mark of authentic Christianity.

3 John 14

A.V.	N.E.B.
14. Peace be to thee.	Peace be with you.

See *Romans* 1 : 7 (pp. 95 ff.)

THE EPISTLE OF JUDE

Jude 2

A.V.

2. Mercy unto you, and peace, and love, be multiplied.

N.E.B.

Mercy, peace, and love be yours in fullest measure.

THIS prayer for 'mercy, peace, and love . . . in fullest measure' (N.E.B.) is similar to the 'grace, mercy, and peace' of 1 *Timothy* 1 : 2 (see p. 160 on 'mercy'). 'Love' here takes the place of 'grace' there, but the two concepts are very close in theological and religious thought; grace being a manifestation of love, an outgoing of the mind and heart of God in redeeming activity.

Jude 24-25

A.V.

24. Now unto him that is able to keep you from falling, and to present you faultless before the presence of his glory with exceeding joy,

25. To the only wise God our Saviour, be glory and majesty, dominion and power, both now and ever. Amen.

N.E.B.

Now to the One who can keep you from falling and set you in the presence of his glory, jubilant and above reproach,

To the only God our Saviour, be glory and majesty, might and authority, through Jesus Christ our Lord, before all time, now, and for evermore. Amen.

This prayer — if such it may be called — is an exclamation, an ascription to God of the honour due to His Name. As with the songs scattered throughout the Book of the Revelation, it is an outburst of devotion, set against a background of darkness and apostasy. In fact, there are few passages in the New Testament where the forces of evil are so vividly described as in this Epistle, which the New English Bible well entitles 'The Danger of False Belief'. Whoever they were whom the writer was addressing, it is clear that they were in imminent danger of being led astray by

'enemies of religion' (v. 4, N.E.B.). But there is no need for them to
go wrong. There is One who can keep them. This is the theme of
these closing verses.

The opening words are identical with those of *Ephesians* 3: 20;
both doxologies move in somewhat similar areas of thought. 'To
the One who is able . . .' In Ephesians, it is 'to do exceeding
abundantly . . .' Here in Jude, it is 'to keep you from falling and to
set you in the presence of His glory, jubilant and above reproach'
(N.E.B.). Jude looks forward to the Day when the secrets of all
hearts shall be disclosed. What will it be—shame or jubilation?
Remorse or no reproach? There are resources in Christ to decide
that question in favour of jubilation and no reproach. There is no
need to stumble. The power of God can keep us unblemished.

THE PRAYERS IN THE REVELATION

Revelation 1: 4-7

A.V.

4. Grace be unto you, and peace, from him which is, and which was, and which is to come; and from the seven Spirits which are before his throne;

5. And from Jesus Christ, who is the faithful witness, and the first-begotten of the dead, and the prince of the kings of the earth. Unto him that loved us, and washed us from our sins in his own blood,

6. And hath made us kings and priests unto God and his Father; to him be glory and dominion for ever and ever. Amen.

7. Behold, he cometh with clouds; and every eye shall see him, and they also which pierced him: and all kindreds of the earth shall wail because of him. Even so, Amen.

N.E.B.

Grace be to you and peace, from him who is and who was and who is to come, from the seven spirits before his throne,

And from Jesus Christ, the faithful witness, the first-born from the dead and ruler of the kings of the earth. To him who loves us and freed us from our sins with his life's blood,

Who made of us a royal house, to serve as the priests of his God and Father—to him be glory and dominion for ever and ever! Amen.

Behold, he is coming with the clouds! Every eye shall see him, and among them those who pierced him; and all the peoples of the world shall lament in remorse. So it shall be. Amen.

THIS greeting-prayer begins in the same way that St. Paul begins many of his letters. But the greeting is very considerably elaborated. *First*, God is described as the one 'who is and who was and who is to come', that is, He is eternal and unchanging. *Secondly*, the greeting comes 'from the seven spirits before His throne'. This phrase anticipates 4: 5, and probably is meant to refer to the Holy Spirit in His manifold activities. *Thirdly*, the greeting comes from Jesus Christ. Appropriately, He is called 'the faithful witness'. This book is addressed to those who would be witnesses to Christ in situations appallingly difficult and testing. The form of the greeting will remind them of One who in His witness to the truth was faithful unto death. More than that, He greets them not as a voice from the dead, but as One who has risen from the dead, the first of a host who in Him will rise. Again, He greets them as One who already is supreme — 'ruler of the kings of the earth'.

The greeting is trinitarian in its form (Father, Spirit, Son), and is followed by an ascription of worship which anticipates the songs which we shall soon be noticing, strung out across the length of the book.

The ascription is addressed to 'Him who loves us' (N.E.B. – the present continuous tense should be noted) 'and freed us . . .' (the past tense no doubt refers to the great act of Christ's self-giving on the cross). This 'freeing' from our sins was at the price of His own blood.

The language of kingship and priesthood with which the Church is described is very closely similar to that of 1 *Peter* 2: 9.

Verse 7 is included in this section because, though the major part of it is a statement of fact and hope, its closing words ('So it shall be. Amen') virtually turn it into a prayer. They make us look Godwards. 'Amen' indicates the meditative gladness of assent (see *St. Matthew* 6: 13; p. 41).

The verse is generally taken as referring to the future Advent of Christ, though some take it to refer to the constant coming of Jesus, veiled from ordinary sight but revealed to believers (so Erskine Hill, *Mystical Studies in the Apocalypse*, pp. 162 ff.).

The Songs

Strung throughout the Book of the Revelation is a series of songs. Perhaps they could be called prayers inasmuch as they are addressed to Deity, and therefore they should be mentioned in this book. It will be best to deal with them all together, for there is a certain sameness about them. It might be more accurate to call them hymns of praise rather than prayers – Professor C. F. D. Moule describes them as 'Psalm-like . . . ejaculations of worship . . . splendid Christian enthronement Psalms'. He adds: 'It is hard to doubt that they represent the kind of poetry which Christians actually used in corporate worship . . . It is to liturgy that we are able to trace the genesis of such parts of the New Testament – and to liturgy deeply influenced by Jewish forms' (*The Birth of the New Testament*, p. 23).

'Enthronement Psalms' – the phrase is a good one. The Book of the Revelation is a difficult book, and one cannot here begin to write a commentary on it[1]. Suffice it to say that it was written for a Church going through a period of distress and persecution; written to maintain that God's purposes could not be defeated by man's evil machinations. His coming reign, and with it the triumph of good over evil, was assured. Therefore the Church, insignificant as it was in the eyes of men, persecuted and battered, could *sing*! Let its members, concerned though they naturally were with things temporal, look up – up to the Throne of God and of the Lamb. And as they looked up, let them worship and adore. Let them join in the never-ceasing worship of those who have gone on before, who serve God day and night in His holy temple. With them they are one, because they are one with Him.

Our best method will be to set out these songs (side by side in the Authorised Version and in the New English Bible) as we have done with the other prayers of the New Testament, and to interrupt the reading of them only with the minimum of comment:

Revelation 4: 8, 11

A.V.	N.E.B.
8. Holy, holy, holy, Lord God Almighty, which was, and is, and is to come.	'Holy, holy, holy is God the sovereign Lord of all, who was, and is, and is to come!'
11. Thou art worthy, O Lord, to receive glory and honour and power: for thou hast created all things, and for thy pleasure they are and were created.	'Thou art worthy, O Lord our God, to receive glory and honour and power, because thou didst create all things; by thy will they were created, and have their being!'

This should be linked with the three songs recorded in the next chapter, for chapters 4 and 5 are a unity within the Book.

Revelation 5: 9-10, 12, 13

A.V.	N.E.B.
9. Thou art worthy to take the book, and to open the seals thereof: for thou wast slain, and hast redeemed us to God by thy	'Thou are worthy to take the scroll and to break its seals, for thou wast slain and by thy blood didst purchase for God men of

[1] Perhaps I may refer to the chapter, 'The Seer of the Revelation', in my *Five Makers of the New Testament*, pp. 59-96, for a brief introduction to the book.

A.V.   N.E.B.

blood out of every kindred, and   every tribe and language, people
tongue, and people, and nation;   and nation;

10. And hast made us unto our   Thou hast made of them a royal
God kings and priests: and we   house, to serve our God as priests;
shall reign on the earth.   and they shall reign upon earth.'

12. Worthy is the Lamb that was   '. . . Worthy is the Lamb, the
slain to receive power, and riches, Lamb that was slain, to receive all
and wisdom, and strength, and   power and wealth, wisdom and
honour, and glory, and blessing.   might, honour and glory and
                                     praise!'

13. . . . Blessing, and honour, and '. . . Praise and honour, glory and
glory, and power, be unto him   might, to him who sits on the
that sitteth upon the throne, and   throne and to the Lamb for ever
unto the Lamb for ever and ever.   and ever!'

The Seer in his vision sees a door opened in heaven. He is caught
up into heaven and sees the throne of God and the thrones of His
attendant 'elders', seven spirits, four living creatures, all of them
engaged in worship. He listens, and hears *first* the *trisagion* (4: 8,
11), *secondly*, the new song (5: 9-10), *thirdly*, the song of the angels
(5: 12), and *last*, the universal song of all creation (5: 13). All those
whom the Seer depicts are engaged in worship, in adoration, of
God the sovereign Lord and of the Lamb. If we may dare to put it
thus, the Throne is a shared Throne – it is the Throne *of God and
of the Lamb*.

> 'The highest place which heaven affords
> Is His, is His by right.'

To this ascription by all creation (5: 13) of highest honour to the
Lamb all the other 'orders' agree, with their 'Amen' and their
worship (5: 14).

Revelation 7: 10, 12

A.V.   N.E.B.

10. . . . Salvation to our God   '. . . Victory to our God who sits
which sitteth upon the throne, and   on the throne, and to the Lamb!'
unto the Lamb.

12. . . . Amen: Blessing, and   '. . . Amen! Praise and glory and
glory, and wisdom, and thanks-   wisdom, thanksgiving and honour,
giving, and honour, and power,   power and might, be to our God
and might, be unto our God for   for ever and ever! Amen.'
ever and ever. Amen.

Chapter 7 is a parenthesis, a kind of gracious breathing-space in the midst of the depicting of a terrible series of judgements. Chapters 5 and 6 have been occupied with the breaking of six seals which are visions of divine judgement. Before the breaking of the seventh seal comes the vision of the vast throng of those who had the mark of God in their foreheads, martyrs now purified and victorious ('clothed with white robes, and palms in their hands', 7: 9). They, like the others who were described in chapters 4 and 5, are engaged in worship, and again it is worship addressed to God and the Lamb.

Revelation 11: 15, 17-18

A.V.	N.E.B.
15. . . . The kingdoms of this world are become the kingdoms of our Lord, and of his Christ; and he shall reign for ever and ever.	'. . . The sovereignty of the world has passed to our Lord and his Christ, and he shall reign for ever and ever!'
17. . . . We give thee thanks, O Lord God Almighty, which art, and wast, and art to come; because thou hast taken to thee thy great power, and hast reigned.	'. . . We give thee thanks, O Lord God, sovereign over all, who art and who wast, because thou hast taken thy great power into thy hands and entered upon thy reign.
18. And the nations were angry, and thy wrath is come, and the time of the dead, that they should be judged, and that thou shouldest give reward unto thy servants the prophets, and to the saints, and them that fear thy name, small and great; and shouldest destroy them which destroy the earth.	The nations raged, but thy day of retribution has come. Now is the time for the dead to be judged; now is the time for recompense to thy servants the prophets, to thy dedicated people, and all who honour thy name, both great and small, the time to destroy those who destroy the earth.'

The seer, in a burst of prophetic praise, sees the day when the reign of God shall be complete, the sovereignty indeed in the hands of 'our Lord and his Christ', the wrong-doing of the nations punished, the dead judged, the servants of God vindicated. It was precisely this profound eschatological hope which enabled the Church in the first century to endure its terrible persecution. Again and again that experience has been repeated in times of severe trial, and God's servants have been enabled to worship under conditions of great distress.

Revelation 15: 3-4

A.V.

3. . . . Great and marvellous are thy works, Lord God Almighty; just and true are thy ways, thou King of saints.

4. Who shall not fear thee, O Lord, and glorify thy name? for thou only art holy : for all nations shall come and worship before thee; for thy judgments are made manifest.

N.E.B.

'. . . Great and marvellous are thy deeds, O Lord God, sovereign over all; just and true are thy ways, thou king of the ages.

Who shall not revere thee, Lord, and do homage to thy name? For thou alone art holy. All nations shall come and worship in thy presence, for thy just dealings stand revealed.'

Those who chant this song are those who have 'won the victory over the beast and its image, and the number of its name', that is to say, the opposition of the Roman Empire with its imperial priesthood and its emperor-worship. It is the song of Moses and the song of the Lamb. Moses had been the first great deliverer who had brought God's people out of Egypt, through the Red Sea, into the promised land. Now a greater than Moses, Jesus, the Lamb of God, has effected His people's redemption at the price of His own blood. The King of the ages (15: 3) has vindicated His name. All nations shall confess His holiness and truth. (The thought and the language recur in 16: 5-7.)

Revelation 19: 1-8

A.V.

1. . . . Alleluia; Salvation, and glory, and honour, and power, unto the Lord our God :

2. For true and righteous are his judgments : for he hath judged the great whore, which did corrupt the earth with her fornication, and hath avenged the blood of his servants at her hand.

3. . . . Alleluia. And her smoke rose up for ever and ever.

4. . . . Amen; Alleluia.

5. . . . Praise our God, all ye his servants, and ye that fear him, both small and great.

N.E.B.

'. . . Alleluia! Victory and glory and power belong to our God,

For true and just are his judgements! He has condemned the great whore who corrupted the earth with her fornication, and has avenged upon her the blood of his servants.'

'. . . Alleluia! The smoke goes up from her for ever and ever!'

'. . . Amen! Alleluia!'

'. . . Praise our God, all you his servants, you that fear him, both great and small!'

<table>
<tr><td>A.V.</td><td>N.E.B.</td></tr>
</table>

A.V.	N.E.B.
6. . . . Alleluia : for the Lord God omnipotent reigneth.	'. . . Alleluia! The Lord our God, sovereign over all, has entered on his reign!
7. Let us be glad and rejoice, and give honour to him: for the marriage of the Lamb is come, and his wife hath made herself ready.	7. Exult and shout for joy and do him homage, for the wedding-day of the Lamb has come! His bride has made herself ready,
8. And to her was granted that she should be arrayed in fine linen, clean and white.	And for her dress she has been given fine linen, clean and shining.'

Chapters 17 and 18 are unequalled for a description of the forces of tyranny concentrated in Rome. The language is gaudy and vulgar, for that was how Rome appeared to the writer. Now Rome, till recently so prosperous, lies shattered. A great cry of exultation goes up to God – 'Alleluia!' Rome is finished. 'The Lord our God, sovereign over all, has entered on His reign' (19: 6, N.E.B.). The bride, the Church, so long persecuted and forlorn, is ready for her wedding-day with the Lamb.

It will be noted that in vv. 3 and 8 the New English Bible takes more of the words as the 'direct speech' of the Songs than does the Authorised Version.

Revelation 22: 20

A.V.	N.E.B.
20. Even so, come, Lord Jesus.	Amen. Come, Lord Jesus!

In the course of our study of the prayers of the New Testament, we have frequently noticed how strong an influence on life and character was the hope of the coming of Christ to wind up history and inaugurate the consummation of the reign of God. Nowhere is the longing for this advent stronger than in the Book of the Revelation. Through persecution and terror, the members of the young Church had held on to the faith that God reigned. But as yet, as the writer of the Epistle to the Hebrews had said, they did not see 'all things put under Him' (2: 8). That day was yet to come. *He* was yet to come. The book which began with the assertion 'Behold, he is coming with the clouds!' (1: 7) ends with the answer 'Amen' to the assertion 'Yes, I am coming soon!' and with the prayer

'Come, Lord Jesus!' It is a repetition, in Greek, of that liturgical prayer which St. Paul used at the end of his first letter to the Corinthians (16: 22) – 'Marana tha', 'come, O Lord' (see pp. 110 ff.). It is the Christian's response to the Master's warning – 'lest coming suddenly, He find you sleeping' (St. Mark 13: 36).

Revelation 22: 21

A.V.	N.E.B.
21. The grace of our Lord Jesus Christ be with you all. Amen.	The grace of the Lord Jesus be with you all.

See 2 Corinthians 13 : 14 (pp. 117 ff.)

LITANY OF JESUS PRAYING

(see p. 71)

Father, the hour is come; glorify thy Son, that thy Son may glorify thee.
Father in heaven; *Hallowed be thy Name.*

As thou hast given him power over all flesh, that he should give eternal
life to all whom thou hast given him.
Father in heaven; *Hallowed be thy Name.*

And this is life eternal, that they should know thee, the only true God,
and Jesus Christ whom thou hast sent.
Father in heaven; *Hallowed be thy Name.*

I have glorified thee on the earth; I have finished the work that thou
gavest me to do.
Father in heaven; *Hallowed be thy Name.*

And now, Father, glorify thou me with thine own self, with the glory
which I had with thee before the world was.
Father in heaven; *Hallowed be thy Name.*

I have manifested thy Name unto the men whom thou gavest me out of
the world.
Father in heaven; *Thy kingdom come.*

I pray for them; I pray not for the world but for those whom thou hast
given me, for they are thine.
Father in heaven; *Thy kingdom come.*

Holy Father, keep in thy Name those whom thou hast given me, that
they may be one, even as we are one.
Father in heaven; *Thy kingdom come.*

These things I speak in the world, that they may have my joy fulfilled in
themselves.
Father in heaven; *Thy kingdom come.*

I have given them thy word; and the world hath hated them because
they are not of the world, even as I am not of the world.
Father in heaven; *The kingdom come.*

I pray not that thou shouldest take them out of the world, but that thou shouldest keep them from the evil.
Father in heaven; *Thy will be done.*

They are not of the world, even as I am not of the world.
Father in heaven; *Thy will be done.*

Sanctify them in the truth; thy word is truth.
Father in heaven; *Thy will be done.*

As thou hast sent me into the world, even so have I sent them into the world.
Father in heaven; *Thy will be done.*

And for their sakes I sanctify myself, that they also may be sanctified in the truth.
Father in heaven; *Thy will be done.*

Neither do I pray for these alone, but for them also who shall believe on me through their word.
Father in heaven; *Thy will be done.*

That they all may be one, as thou, Father, art in me, and I in thee.
Father in heaven; *Thy will be done.*

That they also may be one in us, that the world may believe that thou hast sent me.
Father in heaven; *Thy will be done.*

And the glory which thou gavest me have I given them, that they may be one even as we are one.
Father in heaven; *Thy will be done.*

I in them and thou in me, that they may be perfected into one.
Father in heaven; *Thy will be done.*

That the world may know that thou hast sent me and hast loved them as thou hast loved me.
Father in heaven; *Thy will be done.*

Our Father, which art in heaven, Hallowed be thy Name; Thy kingdom come; Thy will be done; In earth as it is in heaven. Give us this day our daily bread. And forgive us our trespasses, As we forgive them that trespass against us. And lead us not into temptation; But deliver us from evil.

Father, I will that they also, whom thou hast given me, be with me where I am, that they may behold my glory which thou hast given me.
For thine is the kingdom, the power, and the glory, for ever and ever.

For thou lovedst me before the foundation of the world.
For thine is the kingdom, the power, and the glory, for ever and ever.

O righteous Father, the world hath not known thee, but I have known thee; and these have known that thou hast sent me.
For thine is the kingdom, the power, and the glory, for ever and ever.

And I have made known unto them thy Name, and will make it known, that the love with which thou hast loved me may be in them, and I in them.
For thine is the kingdom, the power, and the glory, for ever and ever.
Amen.

A Prayer

Holy Father, whose blessed Son prayed not only for his chosen twelve, but for them also who were to believe on him through their word, that they all might be one; Grant that as thou, Father, art in him and he in thee, they also may be perfected into one, that the world may know that thou dost love thy Church as thou dost love thy Son; who now liveth and reigneth with thee and the Holy Ghost, ever one God, world without end. *Amen.*

INDEX OF AUTHORS

75 76 77 10 9 8 7 6 5 4 3 2 1